I'M A MOM:

Meditations

for New Mothers

ST. CATHERINE'S HOSPITAL

3556 Seventh Avenue
Kenosha, Wisconsin 53140-2595
Telephone (414) 656-3011

Caring for Generations

Also by Ellen Sue Stern

I Do:
Meditations for Brides

I'm Having a Baby:
Meditations for Expectant Mothers

Running on Empty:
Meditations for Indispensable Women

Shortchanged:
*What You Gain When You Choose to
Love Him . . . or Leave Him*

Expecting Change:
The Emotional Journey Through Pregnancy

The Indispensable Woman

I'M A MOM:
Meditations for New Mothers

•

Ellen Sue Stern

A DELL TRADE PAPERBACK

A DELL TRADE PAPERBACK

Published by
Dell Publishing
a division of
Bantam Doubleday Dell Publishing Group, Inc.
1540 Broadway
New York, New York 10036

The trademark Dell® is registered in the U.S. Patent and Trademark Office.

ISBN: 0-440-50456-2

Printed in the United States of America

Published simultaneously in Canada

July 1993

10 9 8 7 6 5 4 3 2

FFG

This book is dedicated
with great love
to my sister, Faith.

ACKNOWLEDGMENTS

I wish to thank the following individuals for your support and encouragements:

Zoe and Evan Stern: for being such fabulous children.
Joey Morris: for your love.
Trish Todd and Betsy Bundschuh: for superb editorial help.
Gary Stern: for, once again, contributing your time and energy.

INTRODUCTION

Motherhood is the most universal experience women share. Yet, if you asked a hundred different women to talk about what it's really like to be a mother, you'd likely hear a hundred varying—and seemingly contradictory—descriptions:

"Being a mom is exciting," says one woman. "It's incredibly boring and monotonous," says another. One says, "It's the easiest, most natural thing in the world." Another replies, "It's the single hardest thing I've ever done."

Yet through all these descriptions runs a common thread—and that common thread is intensity. Whether mothers talk about anticipation or apprehension, hopes or fears, the moments of bliss or the times of simply getting through another day, most women say motherhood is a profound and intensely emotional experience.

Another thing most women agree on is that in many ways motherhood is a solitary journey. Regardless of how wide our circle of support, the memorable moments of joy—when our baby first smiles, walks, and says mommy—along with the inevitable struggles and heartaches—when our child is sad, sick or hurt—are often celebrated or struggled through alone. Which is why I've written *I'm a Mom: Meditations for New Mothers* as a daily companion to help guide, inspire, support, and reassure you along every step of the way.

This book is not meant as childrearing advice, but rather as a spiritual companion to help you reflect on the meaning of this experience in your life. You may choose to follow each page chronologically; you may want to flip through randomly, landing wherever is relevant at any given time. You may wish to use these meditations as a springboard for keeping a "mother's journal" or as a way to facilitate conversations with your mate or moms' group.

However you choose to make use of this book, know that it is written with gratitude and respect. Gratitude for the opportunity to share—in some small way—the trials and triumphs of motherhood. And respect for the incredible contribution each of us is making to our families, communities, and in the world.

Writing this book has been a bittersweet trip back in time to when my children, now eight and ten, were small. Looking back, I yearn for the softness and sweetness of a time now long past. And, I realize with pride and pleasure how much more I have to look forward to as they and I continue to grow.

Because ultimately growth is what motherhood is about. As we care for our children, we learn the importance of caring for ourselves, balancing all the competing demands in our busy schedules. As we strive to impart our ethics, we continually reevaluate our own values, refine our goals, and recommit to what's truly important in our lives. And, as we nurture our children's spirit, our own spirituality deepens and grows.

All of this takes time. We don't become mothers overnight, but rather little by little, over days, months, and years. It is my hope that this book will be a helpful companion as you embark on this challenging, life-changing journey.

Birth Day

Oh, baby. Come closer. Eye to eye, soul to soul. Come say hello to your new-born mother.
Phyllis Chesler

WELCOME! Welcome to your baby! Welcome to motherhood!

For nearly a year you have anticipated meeting your child. Now that day has finally arrived. As you hold your baby in your arms, look deeply into his or her eyes. Look with joy, with gratitude for having reached this wondrous moment. Share your fears, hopes, and dreams for the future.

You have so much to look forward to. So much to learn. So much to do as you bring your child home and begin your new life together.

This is indeed a new day. A day of celebration. A fleeting, unforgettable time in which newborn and mother finally meet.

Affirmation: I celebrate the beginning of a new life.

The First Cry

Your baby's first cry is the one you hear in the delivery room, the triumphant, tension-shattering sound that says, "I'm here, I'm breathing, I'm alive!"
Katherine Karlsrud

Thank God!! That first wonderful cry!!

Never before has the sound of a cry been so heartily welcomed, so deeply reassuring. No matter how many times we heed our child's cry and soothe his tears in the years to come, no cry ever holds so much promise and so much pleasure.

Following the prophetic cry we wait anxiously for the results of the Apgar test—the first formal measurement our baby is given. Some babies score high, while others take a little time to recover from birth, which is why the Apgar is repeated after fifteen minutes.

Like in most tests, the numbers mean less than our own personal assessment as we stroke our newborn's perfect skin, count fingers and toes, and with great relief give thanks for our child's health and well-being.

Affirmation: Thank God you're here.

Cutting the Cord

The broken cord may yet be joined again
But in the midst a knot will yet remain.
Anwari-i sueill

It is a powerful, poignant moment when the umbilical cord is cut. For nine months we are bonded through tissue and vessel with our baby; now we are each on our own.

The symbolism of cutting the cord is vivid. We've reached the moment of separation, of cutting loose. Of accepting our child's entrance into the world as a singular, independent individual.

Yet the cord is never completely severed. We feel the tug when our baby inconsolably cries with colic and we would do anything to take away the pain. We feel the knot of motherhood every single time our child turns to us and says, "I hurt, Mommy. Fix it."

My children, eight and ten, ride off on their bicycles, go to school, go away to camp. Yet there are moments when they curl back into my arms, almost as if to reconnect the cord. We are forever tied.

Affirmation: The mother-child knot is forever.

Weight Loss

> *I was so thankful not to be pregnant anymore, I laughed and stroked my body which now only belonged to me once again.*
> Jane Lazarre

What an amazing feeling! To slowly rub our hand over our almost-flat tummy (at least by comparison!). To lie on our stomach, easily bend over to tie our shoes, and gradually ease back into our prepregnancy jeans.

The operative word here is *gradually*. Although most women experience a significant drop in weight following delivery, those last ten or fifteen pounds can be excruciatingly slow to go. Don't be disappointed if your stomach looks like crepe paper or all that fit are your early maternity clothes. With a healthful diet, exercise, and time the extra weight will eventually disappear.

While reclaiming your body you may experience a mixture of sadness and delight: feelings of emptiness where the baby once was; pleasure at new lightness and freedom of movement.

Meanwhile be easy on yourself. It took nine months for your baby to grow. Give yourself at least that much time to get back in shape.

Affirmation: I will be patient as my body recovers.

Fear

I remember leaving the hospital thinking, "Wait, are they going to let me just walk off with him? I don't know beans about babies!"

Anne Tyler

That's exactly how I felt after my daughter, Zoe, was born. I had never fed or diapered a baby before, never even held one for longer than two minutes; the idea of being totally responsible for her was nothing short of terrifying.

Here's what I discovered: Those first twenty-four hours are trial by fire. At four A.M., when the baby's screaming to be fed ("Didn't we just feed him? . . . Oh, I'm too tired to remember!") and we're fumbling in the dark for a diaper, we figure out real fast what to do and how to do it.

While the first few days may be rough, within a week we're bona-fide experts. But don't hesitate to ask for help. There are lots of resources to turn to—friends, neighbors, mothers and mothers-in-law, books, a home health nurse—all can provide support as we learn how to care for our baby.

Affirmation: I'm learning on the job.

Intimacy

> *In the sheltered simplicity of the first days after a baby is born, one sees again the magical closed circle . . . of two people existing only for each other.*
> Anne Morrow Lindbergh

The intimacy between mother and child goes beyond closeness, beyond comfort, beyond caring. It is a bond so infinite, so impenetrable, we sometimes forget anyone or anything else exists.

In the first weeks of motherhood make sure to give yourself lots of time alone with your baby, time to rock and cuddle, time to count fingers and toes—over and over—time for just the two of you to be wrapped up in your own little world.

It's also important to open the circle to others so that you don't become isolated. Relish the sweet and magical intimacy between you and your child. But be sure to also invite your mate, older children, extended family and friends to bond with the baby and give you the nurturing and companionship you need.

Affirmation: This is a magical time for my baby and me.

Memories

I think of my children's births—carry them around with me every day of my life.
Joyce Maynard

A mere few months ago you were anxiously awaiting your due date, practicing breathing, timing contractions, and pushing through with every ounce of strength and stamina to win the marathon of a lifetime.

Now that the baby's here, your attention is focused elsewhere. Time goes by in a blur of sleepless nights, endless changing, feeding, bathing, and your baby's birth fades into the background. It begins to seem like a remote dreamscape (or awful nightmare, depending on how things went).

It's important to hold on to your birth experience and commit it to a special place in your memory. The same courage you summoned during childbirth will serve you well as you meet the staggering challenges of motherhood. Take a moment now to recall how it felt to give birth to your child. Remember your pain. Your joy. Your triumph.

Affirmation: I will always remember what it took to give birth to my child.

Emotions

> *There aren't words yet invented to define the emotions a mother feels as she cuddles her newborn child.*
> Janet Leigh

Awed. Overwhelmed. Flooded with tenderness the likes of which we never guessed.

None of these words entirely describes the waves of emotion we feel as we hold our baby in our arms. Such deep and boundless love. Such passionate commitment. And so much at stake.

Although you may tell your child how much you love her every day forever, it's impossible completely to convey the pure emotional intensity experienced in the early weeks of motherhood.

Invest in a journal and write down your feelings, now, while they're fresh. Or write a letter to your child, one that will serve as a keepsake of the first, precious days of your life together.

Affirmation: I love you more than words can say.

Advice

As time passes, we all get better at blazing a trail through the thicket of advice.

Margot Bennet

And is there ever a lot of advice out there! Parenting manuals with tried-and-true tips on child rearing. Experienced, well-meaning friends and relatives. Even your co-workers and neighbors may feel compelled to offer words of wisdom—with or without your asking.

Some advice is helpful. Some is irrelevant. And some is just static interference that makes you feel defensive or pressured about being a good enough parent.

Here's one more piece of unsolicited advice: Listen carefully, then trust your gut. Ninety-nine percent of the time, when it comes to your baby, you know best. There's a ton of information, yet no clear-cut manual for mothering. Whether you're trying to decide when it's time to introduce rice cereal, if it's okay to use a playpen, or whether to opt for home or institutional child care, consider your child's needs and preferences, make the most informed decision possible, and don't let other people's opinions sway your confidence.

Affirmation: Mother knows best.

Admiration

> *Parents of young children should realize that few people, and maybe no one, will find their children as enchanting as they do.*
>
> *Barbara Walters*

I still haven't quite figured this out, as evidenced by the pile of dog-eared photographs of my children I insist on pulling out of my purse and shoving under the noses of utter strangers at dinner parties.

Inevitably I'm insulted when they're dismissed with a cool glance and polite acknowledgment instead of the oohs, ahhs, and "Shouldn't they model?" comments I expect.

Although it's taken nearly eleven years, I'm beginning to catch on. Everyone thinks their children are the most gorgeous, the most brilliant, the most talented. And no one else is as captivated by our child as we are.

Sad but true, we may get more rave reviews on the new bathroom wallpaper than on our baby's breathtaking face. Except when grandparents arrive. Now, there's an appreciative audience!

Affirmation: My baby is beautiful.

A Day in the Life

*It's eleven A.M., and the baby finally went down for a nap.
You were up four times during the night and are ready to
collapse. The doorbell rings; it's your mother-in-law. She's
stopped by to visit. What do you do?*

Thank her for coming and ask her to come back when
the baby's up.

Although it's hard to close the door in people's faces—
especially family members who are dying to see the baby
—it's imperative that you don't waste your precious
R-and-R time on visiting. Unless your mother-in-law
has stopped by to stock the refrigerator or throw in three
loads of laundry—in which case you can still lie down
while she does it—be firm about visiting hours. And under no circumstance wake up the baby for viewing. No
matter if your mother-in-law caught the only flight from
Albania, never wake a sleeping baby if you can help it.

If this sounds selfish or rude, remember: Your mother-
in-law can sleep soundly through the night. You need to
replenish your energy for the next round—just a few
short minutes ahead.

Affirmation: I will protect my energy.

Firstborns

> *It is hard to raise sons; and much harder to raise daughters.*
> *Shalom Aleichem*

The fact is it's equally hard—and equally satisfying—to raise sons and daughters, depending on which one you happen to have.

Since I have one of each, I'd venture to say that gender is far less important than personality, and that birth order is perhaps the single most significant element of all.

It *was* harder to raise my daughter than my son, but then she came first. Every move, every decision, every tiny little cry took on tremendous magnitude; we consulted Dr. Spock constantly, called friends to report the first time she rolled over, the first word (*bath*), the first step as if she were Neil Armstrong on the moon.

Yet to be absolutely honest, I can't recall my son, Evan's, first word, and I turned around one day to discover him walking like a pro. As his father, Gary, used to say, "It's a wonder Evan learned anything given how little we worried about it."

Affirmation: Parenthood gets easier with experience.

Bonding

I did not feel anything like the warm bond I was supposed to feel for this bundle newly removed from my body.
Angela Barron McBride

Bonding. That nebulous, all-important attachment we're "supposed" to automatically feel the instant our child is born.

Some women do. For others it takes hours, days, even weeks or months until we feel unequivocally enchanted with our baby.

How quickly we bond depends on lots of things: our birth experience, nursing, our child's gender, along with any number of personal emotional factors. But whether we bond immediately or over time has nothing to do with how much we love our child. I fell in love with Zoe on the spot; it took longer with Evan, yet I grew to adore him every bit as much.

In the end what is known as "bonding" is fairly insignificant. Like any important relationship, real intimacy takes time. Fortunately with our children:

Affirmation: We have years and years to become deeply attached.

Self-acceptance

God couldn't be everywhere, so he (she) invented mothers.
Arabic saying

This is a double-edged sword: On the one hand we're flattered by the idea that motherliness is next to godliness; on the other hand we feel pressured to come up with the superhuman energy, love, and resourcefulness required for the job. It would be great if God dropped by to change a diaper or two.

It's great to have confidence in our ability to handle what comes—whether it's staying up all night nursing a sick baby or summoning our last shred of patience to retrieve the pacifier from under the swing for the four-teenth time. However, we need to keep our expectations in check. Being a mother means being human. Omni-present, yes. Divine, perhaps. But it's just fine to leave a few things off our list. After all, on the seventh day God rested.

Affirmation: I'll do my best.

Preoccupation

When you are a mother, you are never really alone in your thoughts.

Sophia Loren

A corner of our consciousness is always occupied by thoughts of our child. When our infant finally—*finally*—goes down after an arduous four A.M. feeding, we sleep at attention, waiting for him to wake up. We have eyes in the back of our head to spot our toddler as she teeters on the brink of disaster. And a Nobel Prize awaits the mother who invents a way to keep two-year-olds from interrupting the instant the telephone rings.

Even when we're apart from our children, we are "holding them" in our mind. In the middle of a dinner party we run to the phone to call the sitter. In the middle of an important meeting we suddenly remember that we forgot to tell our day-care provider that turnips are out of the question.

Whether we're halfway across town at the grocery store or halfway across the country on a business trip, we worry and wonder if they're happy and safe.

Affirmation: My child is never very far away.

Nursing

A babe at the breast is as much pleasure as the bearing is pain.

> Marion Zimmer Bradley

Here's how different women describe the pleasures of nursing: "exquisitely intimate," "sensual and soothing," "a sense of deep comfort and confidence in providing the best possible start for my child."

Yet nursing can also be difficult and challenging. The anxiety of waiting for milk to come in. Never being sure of whether the baby is getting enough. Being absolutely tied down to the baby's schedule. The physical tenderness and sometimes pain as your newborn suckles at your breast.

For most mothers the satisfaction far outweighs the sacrifice. But nursing isn't the only option. If nursing is going smoothly, great. If you're struggling, give it some time and be gentle with yourself. Combining nursing and bottle-feeding is an alternative, and new formulas on the market resemble breast milk more closely than ever.

Ultimately your health, well-being, and confidence level are more important than whether you bottle-feed or nurse. The pleasures are different, but our babies grow and are nourished either way.

Affirmation: I am a good mother whether I nurse or bottle-feed.

Respect

To nourish children and raise them against odds is, in any time, more valuable than to fix bolts in cars or design nuclear weapons.

    Marilyn French

Many women feel vaguely apologetic about motherhood. I wish this wasn't so. Even though *we* know firsthand how vitally important our role is in nurturing our child, the world still hasn't figured it out. We may feel defensive about choosing to remain home with our child or torn in two directions trying valiantly to balance family and career.

There is no need for apology. No need for defensiveness. There *is*, however, a great need for more respect, support, and appreciation of motherhood. Nothing we ever do, no matter how grand the scale, is more valuable.

Affirmation: Being a mom is an immensely valuable contribution.

Giving

> *While you can quarrel with a grown-up, how can you quarrel with a newborn baby who has stretched out his little arms for you to pick him up?*
> Maria Von Trapp

Sometimes all we can do is throw up our hands and laugh. Or cry. The eighth time we get up in the middle of the night, having fed, diapered, and put the baby back to bed, only to be met with an instant encore of wails, it's tough to feel anything but despair.

These early days are a time of nonstop giving. And giving. Then more giving. With few tangible rewards. At times we feel resentful, and rightfully so. We feel like screaming, "Shut up and go to sleep," but instead we reach down and pick up the baby again.

Eventually we're rewarded. With a smile. A hug from little arms. The blissful morning we awaken to sunshine and suddenly realize our baby has slept through the night.

Affirmation: It will get easier.

Middle-of-the-Night Feedings

I actually remember feeling delight, at two o'clock in the morning, when the baby woke for his feed, because I longed to have another look at him.
Margaret Drabble

In Expecting Change workshops expectant mothers participate in a guided visualization in which they envision life postpartum. What is their perfect fantasy of the first full day at home with their child?

Interestingly, few expectant mothers fantasize about sleeping through the night. In almost every case the great majority look forward to the middle-of-the-night feedings as precious time with their newborn.

I easily understand why. Although sleep is at a premium, there is something incredibly intimate about those middle-of-the-night moments—sitting in utter silence rocking and cuddling as moonlight streams through the window. Few moments with our child are as peaceful and as sweet.

Affirmation: I will savor these moments.

Juggling

A mother could perform the jobs of several air traffic controllers with ease.

                                        Lisa Alther

Have you ever witnessed a group of moms with babies and small children visiting over coffee? It's an amazing scene! Phones ring, Legos fly, "owies" get Band-Aids, and sticky Jell-O fingers get washed and washed again while grown women pick up threads of conversation started fifteen minutes before without skipping a beat.

The ability to do sixteen things at once is cultivated—out of necessity—by moms. It requires these skills: focus, flexibility, and a sense of humor.

Moms-in-action can focus their attention on the most compelling need of the moment, which changes constantly.

Moms-in-action are flexible. They adapt their expectations to reality.

Moms-in-action laugh and keep things in perspective, always prepared to pay attention to something new.

Affirmation: I can keep lots of balls in the air at the same time.

Sensitivity

Because I am a mother, I am capable of being shocked as I never was when I was not one.
Margaret Atwood

"Watching the nightly news—reports of murder, rape, political unrest—disturbs me far more since Lynn was born," says the mother of a six-month-old daughter. Another new mom, watching CNN coverage of hurricane destruction, says, "I couldn't stop crying. I kept thinking about all those families in shelters, homeless and hungry, helpless in the face of such widespread destruction."

Having children increases our sensitivity to pain and suffering. We desperately want our sons and daughters to grow up in a safe world. We agonize over the economy, whether our children will enjoy security and a chance at prosperity. We worry about the environment, the crime rate, the potential for war.

For parents the future is as real as the present. We want to do everything in our power to protect it for our children.

Affirmation: As a mother I am more aware of pain and suffering.

A Day in the Life

You used to have a life. You had friends. Interests. The ability to carry on intelligent conversation. Now you walk around in a daze. You haven't slept, read a newspaper, or been anywhere other than the Quik Shop and the pediatrician's office for a week. You're starting to wonder, When will my life get back to normal?

This is normal. At least for now and the next few months, you may as well resign yourself to a changed reality.

I know, it's frightening. You wanted a baby, but you didn't expect that having one would mean the-end-of-life-as-you-knew-it. What about those magazine articles you read where new mothers lost all their weight in the first week, went back to work in the second, and went out to dinner with friends on the third, where they sipped wine and looked radiant passing around pictures of their lovely baby while catching up on the latest gossip?

Guess what. Those women don't exist. Or if they do, they probably have full-time live-in nannies. Your experience is much more the norm.

Meanwhile here are the guidelines for sanity: Months 1 through 3, don't expect *anything* of yourself other than doing your best to care for your baby. Months 4 through 6, gradually return to work and other activities. By the time your baby is six months old, you'll be amazed at how much your quality of life has improved.

Affirmation: This is my life.

Nagging

I can handle two A.M. feedings, changing diapers, cleaning up vomit and sitting through G-rated movies. What drives me crazy is the nagging.
Linda Henley

It's like having a swarm of gnats buzzing around your head. It's like a migraine headache slowly squeezing your temples like a vise. It's like a bulldozer outside your window when you're trying to sleep.

Nagging (and whining) drives parents crazy. It's one of the most unpleasant parts of dealing with a child, in part because there doesn't seem to be a way to make it stop.

Here's one mother's solution: The first time her child says, "Mommy, I want a cookie" fifteen minutes before dinner, she nicely says no. The second time she firmly says no and warns of a consequence if she's asked again. The third time she sends her child to his room.

Tough love is the perfect solution to nagging. It beats arguing. It beats negotiating. In the long run it beats giving in. And it's the best way to buy a few minutes of peace.

Affirmation: I said no and I mean no.

Letting Go of Control

> *When you have a child, things are unscheduled chaos.*
> Wendy Shulman

We're used to a certain amount of order—operating on a timetable, having things organized, making arrangements and keeping them. Then a baby arrives with the force of a cyclone, disturbing everything in its path.

So we batten down the hatches, remove fragile objects, settle in until the storm passes. It's exciting. Unpredictable. Rarely boring, especially if we can give ourselves over to the chaos.

As a mother of one-year-old twins says, "I had forty-five minutes to get dinner on the table before running off to an important business meeting. The twins wanted to help me make the spaghetti. Can you imagine the mess? I gave in and let them make letters and animals out of the pasta—the kitchen looked like a disaster zone, and I only had five minutes to dress. But I rushed off to my meeting, smiling to myself over what a wonderful time we'd had!"

Affirmation: I will let go of my need for perfect order.

Sleep

There was never a child so lovely but his mother was glad to get him asleep.
Ralph Waldo Emerson

Ahhh. Our children are never more lovely than when they are nestled peacefully under their covers.

Many a new mother, after being yanked through the day by the endless needs of her newborn or toddler, stands adoringly over the crib, admiring her sweet baby in slumber. Those heavy lids; warm, flushed cheeks; and damp, curled fingers wrapped around Teddy Bear are a welcome sight.

In many ways, for new moms sleeptime is the number-one reward. It's when we finally get to sit down, relax, and rest. If we're up for a bonus, we also take a moment to peek at their beds before crawling into our own.

Affirmation: Bedtime eventually comes.

Stickiness

Even when freshly washed and relieved of all obvious confections, children tend to be sticky.
Fran Lebowitz

Truer words were never spoken, literally and figuratively. Children are sticky to pick up, sticky to bring up.

Whether it's using the peanut-butter treatment to get gum out of their hair, extricating them from the branches of a tree, or coming up with age-appropriate answers to questions like "Where do babies come from?" and "Why are we here?" most moms and dads agree that parenting is a constant effort to work our way through sticky situations.

Sometimes the gluey matter is obvious, merely requiring a warm bath and a head-to-toe towel-down. Other times what's sticky is trying to figure out what our child really needs so that we can do our best to prevent them getting seriously stuck somewhere down the road.

Affirmation: I can help smooth the way.

Sharing

The joys of parents are secret, and so are their griefs and fears.
Francis Bacon

So often we keep our parenting triumphs and troubles to ourselves. We censor our desire to exclaim over our child's accomplishments for fear we'll be viewed as bragging or grandiose. Likewise we remain silent on the subject of what's difficult or trying. We think we're the only parent whose baby never sleeps, whose toddler bites, whose two-year-old couldn't be less interested in potty training. We're afraid and ashamed of what other people might think.

In truth all parents are filled with pride at their child's abilities and filled with terror over their seeming failures. So it makes much more sense to support one another instead of isolating ourselves. From the very beginning we can help each other cope when our children struggle and celebrate when they shine, sharing ideas, encouragement, and, most important, simply lending a sympathetic ear.

Affirmation: I needn't be alone in my parenting.

Visitors

> *"Would you like me to make a visit?" asked the home health*
> *aide perkily, calling from the hospital. "Only if you can*
> *baby-sit!" answered the new mom.*
> Ellen Sue Stern

When the call came at nine in the morning, I was wearily sterilizing bottles, staring at last night's dinner dishes in the sink, wearing the same soiled sweatsuit I'd fallen asleep in. The last thing I wanted was an "expert visitor" to chat with. The only thing I did want was someone to take my brand-new baby off my hands so that I could temporarily escape.

Not that the home health aide didn't mean well. And not that she didn't have something to offer. If you have questions, concerns, problems, especially of a medical nature, or simply want reassurance, it's great to have an on-call resource to turn to. But if what you really need is rest and support, you may be better off asking a friend to visit, one who'll wash those dishes or watch the baby while you take a shower or a nap.

Affirmation: I will carefully choose visitors who can be of help.

"Working Mothers"

The phrase "working mother" is redundant.
          Jane Sellman

Every time I hear the words *working mother,* I have to keep myself from throwing a small fit. The term makes me mad. Mad because it implies a distinction between mothers who work inside the home and those who work outside the home. It implies, not too subtly, that mothers at home with their children are not really working, certainly not at a bona-fide career.

In fact all mothers work. The demands of being home all day are no less than, simply different from, the demands of trying to juggle a child and outside career. In some ways being at home is harder. Many women say that going back to work after having a baby is relatively relaxing; it's quieter, more peaceful, and at least you know what to expect.

It's time to eliminate the term *working mother.* The next time you hear someone use it, turn to them and say, "Excuse me, but whatever do you mean?"

Affirmation: All mothers work.

Equal Parenting

> *"Equal parenting" does not work—the maternal fine-tuning never turns off.*
>
> Phyllis Schlafly

While I agree with Schlafly that mothers have a sixth sense when it comes to perceiving their children's needs, I beg to differ with her conclusion that therefore equal parenting is a doomed proposition.

On the contrary, fathers *must* share equal responsibility for their children's care. And mothers must do their part by letting go, stepping aside so that fathers can gain experience—even if it means turning the fine-tuning down a notch.

Ultimately it's more a matter of conditioning than biology. Many modern fathers are every bit as tuned in as their female counterparts. With equal parenting everyone benefits: Fathers enjoy the pleasures of bonding, mothers get a break, and babies get two capable, confident parents.

Affirmation: Let's share the load.

Beginnings

The beginning is the most important part of the work.
Plato

And what a beginning this is. In making the commitment to be a parent, you've already done the earthshaking part. And in some ways this is the decision you really had complete control over.

While parenthood is the greater part of the "work," what happens now that your child is born is somewhat out of your hands. Your child enters the world a distinct individual, whom you can shape but cannot mold to your liking.

Before I had children, I was a great advocate of nurture over nature. Once my children were born, I learned otherwise. Each came out different: Zoe was an "old soul," sensitive, wise, and introspective even as an infant. Evan was as new as the morning's sunrise, fresh, wondrous, filled with innocence and joy.

We begin the "work." Then it becomes our job to help our children become who they already are.

Affirmation: I have given my child a great start. Now I will look forward to discovering who he or she is.

Anxiety

> *I would walk him through the house, weeping with him for my incompetence, for my anxious and jittery soul, which was clearly the wrong style for good mothers.*
> Jane Lazarre

Sometimes nothing seems to work.

We try feeding, rocking, walking in circles till we're ready to collapse, and the baby *still* won't stop crying.

At these moments it's natural to feel incompetent. "If I was really a good mother, I'd know what to do." Right?

Wrong.

Sometimes there's simply nothing to do but wait. It's excruciating and unnerving to listen helplessly when our child appears to be distraught, yet sometimes babies simply cry and cry for no apparent reason.

Try to not take on the blame and remember:

Affirmation: I'm doing everything I can to care for my baby.

Humility

A mother is neither cocky nor proud, because she knows the school principal may call at any minute to report that her child has just driven a motorcycle through the gymnasium.
Mary Kay Blakely

Or snapped the head off a neighbor's priceless porcelain doll. Or stolen a cookie from a toddler in nursery school. Or taunted a child at the school-bus stop, who turns out to be the police chief's daughter.

No matter what age our child is, it's awful when they do something wrong. Especially in public. One of my single worst parenting moments came at a friend's fortieth birthday party when my usually lovely son, Evan, then three, smacked another child across the shoulders with a baseball bat. I've never forgotten the waves of humiliation as every other parent in sight stopped in mid-sentence and stared, shaking their heads at my "bad child" and his "bad mother."

Of course our children aren't actually "bad." Sometimes they just blow it. Then we need to understand what's causing their misbehavior, find appropriate consequences, forgive them, and forgive ourselves.

Affirmation: I am not responsible for my child's occasional outbursts.

Boundaries

> *A child of one can be taught not to do certain things such as touch a hot stove, turn on the gas, pull lamps off their tables by their cords, or wake mommy before noon.*
> *Joan Rivers*

Well, maybe that's asking a little much.

But even a very young child can be taught certain things that make life for you, as a parent, a little bit easier.

For example, it's appropriate to teach a toddler—by using a gate and positive reinforcement—how to avoid tumbling down the steps. And it's possible to teach your one-year-old to remain in her playpen while you grab a quick shower or answer the phone. And, believe it or not, your two-year-old can happily watch a half-hour video while you straighten your house or simply take a break.

Life gets better by inches as your child increasingly gains independence—and you gain much needed respite.

Affirmation: My needs count too.

Anger

Our children will hate us too, y'know.
John Lennon

When my daughter, Zoe, was eighteen months old, she turned to me in fury after being refused a cookie and screamed, "I hate you! I've *always* hated you!"

I didn't know whether to laugh or cry.

It's hard to accept the inevitability that at times our children will feel hatred toward us. The newborn who trustingly wraps his tiny finger around our ear, the two-year-old who hands us a daisy, saying, "You're the best mommy in the world," will eventually also cast powerfully negative emotions in our direction.

There are two ways to protect ourselves when this happens: 1. Remember that it happens to everyone. We, too, at times, felt the same way toward our parents. 2. Remember that our children are separate beings. We don't cause their feelings and we can't control them.

Start now by saying to yourself:

Affirmation: Even when my child hates me, we still love each other deeply.

Permanence

> *You walk in the door of your home, close it to the outside world, and all of a sudden the baby is yours—not on loan from the hospital and definitely not returnable.*
> Ellen Sue Stern

It's a rude awakening. Even though you know at the hospital that the baby is yours (your matching wristbands are proof positive), there's still someone on call 'round the clock to answer questions and run to the rescue.

Suddenly you're on your own. *Really* on your own. It's up to you to figure out what your baby's cries mean, how to get enough breast milk or formula into him, and how best to rock him back to sleep. Of course you're nervous and apprehensive. Contrary to myth, mothering isn't wholly instinctive; a quality performance only comes with experience. And every new mother learns as she goes.

It's a bit of a shock as it sinks in that the baby is *actually* yours and *definitely* here to stay. But with each passing day you will become more and more comfortable.

Affirmation: There is no turning back.

Staying Calm

*The real menace in dealing with a five-year-old is that in no
time at all you begin to sound like a five-year-old.*
Jean Kerr

Or a screaming newborn or toddler.

When our child is upset, when she's whining or crying, it's natural for our response to descend to the same
level. As our patience thins, we lose perspective and find
ourselves in a screaming match that only makes things
worse.

Here's where "Mother's Time-out" comes in handy.
When you feel your blood pressure and temper start to
rise, remove yourself, even if only for a few minutes. Take
a deep breath. Count to ten. Remember that you're a
perfectly reasonable adult trying to cope with a perfectly
unreasonable child.

Recovering your balance—and modulating your voice
—is the best way to comfort your child, and yourself.

Affirmation: This, too, shall pass.

Meals

> *Ask your child what he wants for dinner only if he's buying.*
> Fran Lebowitz

One of the smartest pieces of parenting advice yet!

Too often we feel like a short-order cook: You've defrosted a chicken, but the one-year-old wants pancakes with chocolate chips and the three-year-old insists on macaroni and cheese, hold the cheese, please.

I know. You want to please your child. And of course you want to be sure he eats. But at what cost?

After nearly ten years of catering to my children's culinary capriciousness, I've finally decided to close the restaurant. One meal a night. The "daily special" is reasonable (no stuffed peppers). They eat it, like it or not—or they get themselves a bowl of cereal with milk.

Heartless? Maybe. Hungry? They'll eat.

Affirmation: I have better things to do.

Quality Time

If you want your children to turn out well, spend twice as much time on them and half as much money.
Abigail Van Buren

You may or may not be able to afford designer overalls, gourmet baby food, and the top-of-the-line stroller you admire from a distance at the park.

Unless you have infinite disposable income, throughout parenting there will be times when you say to yourself or to your child, "No. That's something we just can't afford."

When that happens, don't for a minute think you're depriving your child. If anything, you're teaching him the value of money in an honest, loving way.

Ultimately it's your time, attention, and affection that are the real treasures. I have yet to meet anyone with serious complaints that his or her parents didn't buy them enough toys. I've met way too many people still suffering from a shortage of their parents' love.

Affirmation: Love is priceless.

Love

*After the baby was born, I remember thinking that no one had
ever told me how much I would love my child.*
                    Nora Ephron

People probably tried, but it just didn't register. You
listened politely as your best friend bubbled over with her
intense love for her baby. You heard other women go on
and on, extolling the joys of motherhood, and wondered
if they weren't trying to convince themselves of something, or at least exaggerating just a little bit.

They weren't. And they couldn't possibly have made
you understand. Until we are parents, we simply can't
appreciate the depth of passion and protectiveness we feel
toward our child. It's unlike the love we experience in
any other relationship. It floods us with tenderness, over-
whelms us with gratitude.

**Affirmation: Now I know how much I love my
baby.**

Scolding

Some are kissing mothers and some are scolding mothers, but it is love just the same, and most mothers kiss and scold together.

Pearl S. Buck

We've all winced at mothers who seem endlessly to scold and berate their children. But mothers who never criticize, who always shower their children with adoration and approval no matter how they behave, also do a disservice.

There's a place for both scolding and kissing, and the best method is a combination. When we gently but firmly reprimand our child, then fold him into our arms for hugs and kisses, we give this important message: I care enough to discipline you and I love you even when you misbehave.

Affirmation: I will discipline lovingly.

Terror

> *I dream of your sudden death. The stopped breath. The violent choking. The mysterious convulsion.*
> *Phyllis Chesler*

Remember the scene in *Terms of Endearment* where the mother, played by Shirley MacLaine, hysterically climbs into her peacefully asleep newborn's crib and shakes her to make sure she's still breathing?

It's not actually so farfetched. During these first few weeks it's natural to be hypervigilant. Fears of crib death bring us to our baby's side at all hours of the day and night. We study her complexion and count her breaths, terrified of losing what we can barely believe is ours.

We may want to resist the urge to climb *in* the crib, but there's no reason not to stand *by* it until we're absolutely reassured. As the weeks go by, we rest easier, knowing that our baby is okay.

Affirmation: Fears are a natural expression of my love.

A Day in the Life

You lose it. After your son skips his nap, cries all the way to the grocery store, and then reaches out of the cart and pushes two dozen cans of tuna fish off the rack, you scream, "Stop it or I'll never take you anywhere again!" His eyes get huge, and you're horrified at yourself. Whatever got into you? Have you turned into Mommie Dearest?

No. You've simply reached your limit.

It happens to the best of us. No matter how much we love our child, no matter how sincerely we pledge to tread softly, speak quietly, and never, ever scream, there are times when we lose control.

It feels awful. We worry that we've done irreparable damage to our child. So now what do we do?

We can say, "I'm sorry." Even if our child is too young to understand the words, it helps to say, "I'm sorry, I lost my temper. I'll try not to do it again."

Of course you will. If it happens a lot, it may be a sign that you need more support, a less pressured schedule, or possibly some counseling on dealing with anger. If you occasionally lose it, it simply means you're in good company with all the other imperfect parents trying to do their best.

Affirmation: It's acceptable to lose my temper occasionally.

Setting Limits

> *Oh, and at least once a day say "No."*
> Erma Bombeck

It's one of the hardest words in any language for mothers—and one of most useful.

Why is it so hard to say no? Because we're afraid of disappointing our children. We want them to love us. We want to give them everything their hearts desire. And sometimes we just feel like giving up and giving in.

Yet, as Erma Bombeck points out, saying no is fundamental to our child's development, much more important in fact than appeasing them at every turn. Saying "No, you can't cross the street by yourself" to our three-year-old, "No, you can't have M&M's before dinner" to our five-year-old, or "No, you can't watch TV until your homework is finished" to our nine-year-old are all ways of saying we care enough to set limits.

Which won't win us popularity contests in the short run. But this is a loving mother's way of saying *yes* to bigger rewards in the long run.

Affirmation: No can be a way of saying "I love you."

Self-appreciation

Every day, once a day, give yourself a present.
Special Agent Dale Cooper

For Dale Cooper, star FBI agent on television's *Twin Peaks,* the present is likely a great cup of Java, a piece of cherry pie from the Double R Diner, or, if all else fails, there's always a jelly doughnut.

As a mother you deserve at least one present every day. Whether it's a nice hot bubble bath, a bouquet of fresh daisies, or a fifteen-minute break to drink coffee while it's still hot and read the newspaper, it's essential to give yourself something special to help replenish all the energy you expend giving and giving and giving to everyone else in your life.

Affirmation: I deserve a gift.

Independence

> *A mother is not a person to lean on but a person to make leaning unnecessary.*
> Dorothy Canfield Fisher

Right now your baby's dependence on you is absolute. Your constant care and nurturing is literally a matter of life and death.

But before long your task will change. Little by little you shift from twenty-four-hour maintenance to facilitating your child's increasing independence.

Even as your baby, at six months old, begins to sit in a high chair and drink from a bottle, you're challenged to sit back rather than hover over him. As your toddler takes his first steps, you let go, never more than an inch away, praying he won't fall, yet knowing it's inevitable.

Fostering independence is painful. It means watching our children stumble and fail in order that they may stand on their own and succeed.

Affirmation: I will let go a little at a time.

Personal Growth

Parenthood is quite a long word. I expect it contains the rest of my life.

Karen Scott Boates

Which is why we needn't master it all in one day.

We have years, in fact, our whole lifetime, to become better, more effective parents. We learn all the time—from our mistakes, from reading and talking to other parents, and mostly from time spent getting to know our children.

It's true that the first years are the most critical. But each day, each stage of life, is new and provides chances to improve on the past by applying what we've learned.

You're already a better parent than you were two weeks ago. And you'll be a better parent two months and two years from now. But only if you're willing to keep growing on the job.

Affirmation: I have the rest of my life to become the parent I want to be.

Housecleaning

> *The darn trouble with cleaning the house is it gets dirty the next day anyway, so skip a week if you have to. The children are the most important thing.*
> *Barbara Bush*

So often we feel bad for ignoring our children as we rush around the house making beds and folding laundry instead of holding them in our lap cuddling and reading stories.

Yet there's a lot to be said for the peace and order that comes from a reasonably clean house. The chaos of wading through toys and clothes and piles of mail on the sofa makes it harder to concentrate on anything.

So it's a matter of simple choices. Sometimes we have to let the dishes sit in the sink. Other times we have to put the baby in her playpen or the two-year-old in front of the television long enough to straighten up at least.

Whether we put our kids or the laundry on hold momentarily, what's important is to not feel guilty. There's simply too much to do and not enough time to do it.

Affirmation: I'm doing the best I can.

Expectations

Children are likely to live up to what you believe of them.
Lady Bird Johnson

I once saw a child-development expert on television discussing the importance of confidence building. He described his eighteen-month-old daughter perched precariously on the top of their swing set. Instead of shouting "Be careful, you're going to fall!" he calmly repeated to her, "You have perfect balance. You have perfect balance."

I admired his restraint. But his example is tough to follow. It's hard to stay cool when our child is about to drop a pile of plates, tumble off his tricycle, or draw a blank on her first spelling test. Our natural instinct is to warn of imminent danger rather than encourage potential triumph.

Yet the ability to pull through comes partly from the constant building of our children's confidence. When we say "I know you can do it," we give them the extra boost that helps to tip the balance from failure and toward success.

Affirmation: I will have faith in my child's abilities.

Interruptions

> *The quickest way for a parent to get a child's attention is to sit down and look comfortable.*
> Lane Olinhouse

It's like bees to honey. Our children can be happily occupied as long as we're busy making beds or washing dishes, but the instant we call a friend or sit down for a second to catch our breath, they're right in our face, begging for attention.

What's a mother to do?!?

Here's a few strategies to keep your occasional "coffee breaks" relatively disturbance-free: 1. *Go into another room.* Even a newborn can be secure in her crib or bassinet while you steal a few moments alone in your bedroom or the bathroom. 2. *Take regular breaks.* Any child over the age of one can—and must—understand the words "Mommy's taking a rest now. I'll play with you in five minutes." 3. *Be firm.* Giving in seems like the path of least resistance, but there's a price. Unless you establish your right to privacy, your children will continue to interrupt your precious few moments of peace.

Affirmation: I will take an occasional break.

Self-actualization

*My mother wanted me to be her wings, to fly as she never
quite had the courage to do.*
              Erica Jong

We must have the courage to live our own lives fully,
rather than living through our children.

When we put our own aspirations on hold, we set our
children up. Consciously or unconsciously, we expect
them to realize our lost dreams and thwarted ambitions;
the race we never ran translates into intense pressure for
our six-year-old to make the Little League team. The
book we never wrote, the modeling career we were too
afraid to try, carry over into the next generation as we
pressure our kids to be everything *we* wanted to be.

Even as we begin mothering, we must be careful to
follow our dreams and free our children to follow their
own.

Affirmation: I will not live through my children.

Conditioning

> *So I didn't bake cookies. You can buy cookies, but you can't buy love.*
>
> Raquel Welch

For many of us images of mother-love are intimately blended with memories of meat loaf, apple pie, and other culinary affections. Although my own mother worked full-time and hardly ever baked, I still recall with pleasure the one time I came home from school to the pungent aroma of fresh gingerbread cooling on the counter. Even those of us who grew up post–*Donna Reed* were—and still are—inundated with TV commercials in which motherhood is synonymous with fresh-baked cookies hot out of the oven.

The difference is, today's TV moms use Hamburger Helper, slice and bake cookies, and instant mashed potatoes ready in just a minute and a half.

And it's just fine. Because our children don't care whether it's from scratch or magically microwaved. As long as it's made with love.

Affirmation: I don't have to be a TV mom.

Returning to "Work"

*I did not fear being able to work again so much as never
wanting to work again.*
Jane Lazarre

Although many new moms can't wait to return to their
job, others can't imagine trading the gentle rhythm of
mothering for the pressured pace of the workplace.

The idea of returning to the world of nine-to-five may
put you into a mild state of panic. You may worry that
your ambition has permanently vanished, that your mind
has turned to mush, that you couldn't possibly concentrate—much less care—about anything other than your
baby.

Never fear. Most mothers say that their drive and their
ability to focus returns naturally as they ease back into the
job. Although you may never again care about your work
with the single-mindedness you did before, little by little
you will come to enjoy the complementary pleasures of
motherhood and career.

**Affirmation: I will find the right balance between
motherhood and career.**

Vocabulary

> *The beginning of wisdom is to call things by their right names.*
>
> > *Chinese proverb*

It's not too early to begin introducing your child to the proper names for all of his or her anatomy.

Although euphemisms abound—*potty* for toilet, *wee-wee* for urination, *private parts* for penis or vagina—many contemporary parents are opting for the right names right from the beginning. And recent studies suggest that children who are given correct vocabulary rather than cute names grow up more comfortable with their bodies, more candid and confident in their sexuality.

There's nothing to be squeamish or embarrassed about. Consider it part and parcel of your child's education.

Affirmation: I will teach my children to be comfortable with their bodies.

Child Care

*There is not even a name for what I am searching for.
Nanny? Too starchy and British. Sitter? Too transient to
describe someone who (please God) shows up every morning.
Mother? Bite your tongue!*
            Anna Quindlen

Child care. The ultimate struggle and salvation of every
mother who works outside the home.

There really isn't an adequate job title for the position.
What word could possibly describe what we're looking
for? A warm and nurturing individual who will love our
children as much as we do. A clone of ourselves with the
wisdom of Solomon, the patience of a saint, and the experience of Dr. Spock. Someone dependable and responsible who'll never let us down or leave us in the lurch.

It's a lot to ask. And it's no more than we deserve for
our child's well-being and our own peace of mind. Because there's no greater security than knowing our child
is in good hands.

Affirmation: I'll look until I find the right person.

A Day in the Life

Your mother stops by to visit. First she comments that the baby must be cold wearing only a diaper and undershirt, then she questions your brand of rice cereal, then she takes the baby out of your arms to demonstrate a better way to burp him. You're getting annoyed. In fact you wish she'd disappear off the planet. This is your baby and you're not about to be criticized at every turn!

You're right. But that doesn't necessarily solve your problem.

For centuries mothers have given their daughters advice on parenthood; she probably thinks she's helping, and it won't do either of you any good for you to "throw out the mother with the maternity advice."

Instead try saying calmly, "Thanks, Mom, for your help, but it's important for me to make my own decisions regarding my baby." Let her know that you appreciate her concern—and maybe take her comments into consideration—after all, she may know something you don't know, and even if her advice is outdated, it won't hurt you to listen.

To whatever degree possible, prevent this from becoming a power struggle with your baby as the pawn. Be assertive without being aggressive so that you can both enjoy your new relationship as mother and grandmother.

Affirmation: I will find a way gently to assert myself with my mother.

Simple Pleasures

After years of trial and error I have come to the conclusion that the good mother is the mother who looks her child straight in the eye after being asked, "What can I do?" and says helplessly, "I have absolutely no idea."
Phyllis Theroux

Years ago, with some reticence and a carful of puzzles and games, we took our small children to a friend's cabin on Madeline Island on Lake Superior. There was no TV, no VCR, no shopping mall to amuse and distract them.

Much to our surprise, within an hour of unpacking, the kids disappeared for a while, then reappeared in makeshift "period costumes" and proceeded to present a play. They spent the rest of the weekend quietly reading, collecting rocks, and playing word games, looking for the world like characters out of *Little House on the Prairie*.

That weekend taught me a lot about parenting. Left to their own devices, children come up with more good ideas than we could possibly imagine.

Affirmation: My children can entertain themselves.

Supermom

> *I know that somewhere there must be mothers who in one week go back to their regular clothes; who appear at their desks as if nothing happened, whistling.*
> *Phyllis Chesler*

Where?

Here is yet another myth of motherhood that creates intense pressure, guilt, and the feeling that we're simply not on a par with supermom just up the block.

Forget it. If your baby is under three months and you're already back on the job, give yourself a gold star simply for showing up. If your child is under one year of age and you get to work on time more or less regularly with matching shoes and a slight semblance of order on your desk, you deserve a medal.

It requires great organization, brains, and the ability to occasionally be two places at once to balance a family with a career, especially at the beginning. Don't make it harder on yourself by trying to live up to an impossible ideal.

Affirmation: I don't have to compete with anyone.

Protectiveness

I used to be a reasonably adventurous person before I had children; now I am constantly afraid that a low flying aircraft will drop on my children's school.
Margaret Drabble

When it comes to our children, we tread a fine line between responsible protectiveness and obsessive overprotectiveness that makes us crazy and prevents our children from developing their independence.

We shudder at the thought of anything happening to our babies, but we can't lock them in their rooms until they're twenty, either, hoping to keep them from harm's way.

While there's no way to eliminate worry altogether, there *are* ways to keep overprotectiveness in check: by keeping our imagination from running away with us, by having faith in our children's resiliency, and by repeating to ourselves:

Affirmation: I will do everything in my power to protect my child.

Lullabies

> *They sang the way parents have always sung to their children —to lull them and soothe them and most of all, to drown them out.*
>
> *Sherril Jaffe*

Rock-a-bye baby in the treetop . . .

We serenade our children with the lullabyes our parents sang to us as we were drifting off. My eighty-year-old mother-in-law still croons "The Sandman Song" to my children when they sleep at her house, just as she once did to lull their father to sleep.

Sometimes simple lullabyes do the trick; other times our children call for another verse, a bedtime story, a sip of water to calm their restlessness and help ease them into slumber. A musical mobile or night-light helps. But ultimately nothing comforts our child like the sound of our voice singing to them from out of the dark.

Affirmation: My voice is music to my child's ears.

Flexibility

You learn never to count on anything being the same from day to day, that he will fall asleep at a certain hour or sleep for a certain length of time.

Lydia Davis

In Expecting Change workshops expectant mothers play the Baby Reality Game, a board game that simulates the first few weeks of motherhood.

Participants roll the dice to determine their single most important asset: *naps*. If, how long, and how often a newborn naps separates the rested from the ragged, the patient from the irritable, the relatively sane new mothers from those on the verge of a nervous breakdown.

In reality it's often even-odds dice whether or not the baby goes down. We save the shower, phone calls, and mountains of laundry, anticipating a solid two hours of whirlwind activities, then the baby wakes up after fifteen minutes. Or we're sure we can only count on a half hour, so we don't bother to lie down ourselves, then the baby sleeps three and a half and we've missed our window of opportunity.

Since naps are highly unpredictable, it's best to assume the worst and do whatever is highest on the priority list. For most new moms it's sleep. Get it while you can.

Affirmation: I will adjust my priorities realistically.

Fathers

> *It's the men who are discriminated against. They can't bear*
> *children. And no one is likely to do anything about that.*
> Golda Meir

Who knows? Perhaps someday in the future even that
will be possible.

But until such dubious advances come to be, pregnancy and childbirth remain limited to women, while
parenthood is an equal opportunity employer.

It is with great pleasure that I observe a growing movement of men fully involved in raising their children: fathers feeding and diapering newborns, fathers tucking
toddlers into bed, fathers caring for their children (rather
than "baby-sitting" them), fathers picking up children at
day-care centers and showing up for the PTA.

This is a significant step forward. In the long run, fathers carrying their babies in Snuglis matters more than
carrying them in the womb.

**Affirmation: Fathers can do almost everything
mothers can do.**

Ingenuity

Do not, on a rainy day, ask your child what he feels like doing, because I assure you that what he feels like doing, you won't feel like watching.
Fran Lebowitz

Rainy days with babies and small children can be a disaster or a delight, depending on your attitude. It's easy to feel trapped with crabby kids climbing the walls and complaining that there's nothing to do. You can wait for the rain to stop, or you can take this opportunity to tap your creativity.

Art projects, storytime, even housecleaning can be made into a game with prizes for finishing first. Or you can muster your spirit of adventure, pull on galoshes and ponchos, and go for a walk in the puddles.

Much of mothering comes down to inventiveness in the face of adversity, turning drizzly days into warm, memorable ones.

Affirmation: I will use my imagination.

Sibling Rivalry

> *It goes without saying that you should never have more children than you have car windows.*
> Erma Bombeck

If you're a veteran mother, then you may be coping with signs of sibling rivalry. Your three-year-old screams for a Band-Aid just as you begin to nurse the baby. Or your one-year-old wants the only toy his older sister is clutching in her hand. Or both older siblings insist on sitting in the grocery cart, the only place that the infant car seat is secure.

With more than one child motherhood requires artful negotiation. We want to be fair, we want to keep peace, and beyond all else we want each of our children to get what they need.

Here's where situational ethics enters into the equation: At any given moment you need to make the best possible decision for everyone, including *you*. Sometimes the baby's needs prevail, sometimes the older child needs attention while the infant waits, and sometimes you need simply to do whatever will make it easiest on yourself, which might mean hiring a sitter and going to the grocery store alone.

Affirmation: I can't always please everyone.

Devotion

*Your children are always your "babies," even if they have
gray hair.*

        Janet Leigh

We never, ever stop caring for and worrying about our
children. The specifics simply change over time.

The intense caregiving of early motherhood turns into
the constant supervision of toddlers, which gives way to
the mentoring of school-age children, which evolves into
the guiding of our adolescents as they begin the gradual
journey into adulthood.

At each stage we are needed, only in different ways. At
this early stage our relationship is absolutely symbiotic,
more so than at any other time in our children's lives.
Gradually we separate and increasingly care for our children from afar. But no matter how old and gray they get
(and we'll get plenty of gray hairs ourselves in the process), we will always be their mommies and they will
always be our babies.

Affirmation: Motherhood is forever.

Shlepping

> *A suburban mother's role is to deliver children obstetrically once, and by car forever after.*
> Peter De Vries

Some of the nicest times with our children take place while driving in the car. For one thing they're captive; we're assured they're not about to crawl into the garbage or tumble down the stairs. For another thing *we're* captive; our attention isn't torn between them and all the million other things we have to do.

As most moms learn, car motion is often the best way to lull a newborn (I've known more than one mother who drove up and down her driveway just to get her baby to sleep). And some of the best, most spontaneous conversations with small children take place in transit. "What does the Tooth Fairy do with the teeth?" "Why did you marry Daddy?" and "Where does the sky stop?" are some of the topics I've been treated to over the years.

Like many things, kids in cars can be frustrating or fun. It all depends on how you navigate it.

Affirmation: I will make the most of every opportunity to share with my child.

Challenges

A woman who can cope with the terrible twos can cope with anything.

Judith Clabes

And a woman who can cope with labor and delivery can cope with anything. And a woman who can cope with getting up all night with a newborn can cope with anything. And a woman who can cope with chasing after a toddler can cope with anything . . .

Although the "terrible twos" have an especially rough reputation, there are intense challenges at every juncture of motherhood. The stamina, patience, and inner peace required to make it from two to three are no more, no less than what's needed from conception to birth, from birth to two, and from two all the way on up.

At each stage we learn how much we are capable of. And at each stage we stretch a little more.

Affirmation: I'm up to the task.

Tenderness

> *I stumble into the nursery, pick up my son . . . and as he fastens himself to me like a tiny sucking minnow, I am flooded with tenderness.*
> Sara Davidson

We are overwhelmed with tenderness at our newborn's delicacy, dependency, and trust.

No matter how tired we are, no matter how many times we've stumbled in the darkness to heed his tireless cry to be fed, there's something profoundly moving in that instant when our bodies reconnect.

Which isn't to say that we always feel happy, fulfilled, or even willing to nurse. There are times when we're too worn out, too depleted to care. But even then we find the strength to offer sustenance and are deeply satisfied by our ability to nourish our child.

Affirmation: I am moved by tenderness toward my child.

Legacies

Nearly every day an echo of my mother's mothering wafts by me, like the aroma of soup simmering on a stove down the street.

Anna Quindlen

Our mothers' words ring in our ears: "Lay the baby on her stomach to avoid gas." "If you eat that cookie, you'll ruin your appetite." "Don't wear your jacket inside or you'll get overheated." "Now, that's my nice girl!"

It's eerie to find ourselves sounding like our mothers, especially when it's remarks we railed against in our youth. Some of their mothering was wonderful, footsteps worthy of following. In other ways we prefer to forge a new path, free of their influence, truer to our own values and beliefs.

Whether we emulate them or veer from their example, our mothers are our first role model, and their words and actions continue to resonate throughout our lives.

Affirmation: Here are three positive things I learned from my mother about parenting:

1. _____.
2. _____.
3. _____.

Perfectionism

> *There comes a time in all children's lives when they notice that their families aren't perfect.*
> *Phyllis Theroux*

What's perfect? An idyllic childhood in which nothing ever goes wrong? Knees never skinned, Popsicles on demand, parents who never lose their patience, who are always cheerful and energetic, who don't make mistakes and have answers for every problem in the universe?

No. Even if it were possible, it wouldn't make for a perfect childhood. On the contrary, the healthiest families are those in which children are exposed to reality and given tools for coping with hard times—from allowing our young children to see us when we're ill, to saying "No, we can't afford that toy," to helping them through a grandparent's death.

Because life is filled with ups and downs. Teaching our children to weather them is the most "perfect" way to prepare them for what's ahead.

Affirmation: I will relinquish my fantasy of the perfect family.

A Day in the Life

It's been one of those days when you wish you could clone yourself. You've been going since six A.M., when the baby woke screaming with an earache. You've made a trip to the pediatrician's, two runs to the drugstore, burned a batch of brownies, fielded four calls from your mother, and the baby still hasn't napped. You're ready to snap when your husband saunters in at six o'clock and innocently says, "Boy, did I have a hard day at work! So what did you do with yourself all day?"

Before you throw the baby—and everything else in sight—at him, take a deep breath and count to five. Then calmly place *his* child in his arms, announce you're on break for the next half hour, and go soak in a long, hot bath.

Unless he's sharing parental leave, taking full charge of the baby while you're away, the baby's father probably doesn't comprehend how exhausting a job it is. Which doesn't mean you need to throw a fit or go on strike to get your message across. Simply describe the details of your day without either embellishing or diminishing how hard you work and how much you do. If he still doesn't get it, tell him you're taking next Saturday off. He's in charge, you'll be home by six.

Affirmation: I will patiently educate my child's father.

Baby-sitters

> *As I was leaving, Sara said, "It will be okay, Mrs. Stern. Don't worry about a thing." Don't worry? YOU don't worry, I thought to myself. This isn't just ANY baby! She's special!*
>
> Ellen Sue Stern

Of course she is! And of course it's terrifying the first times we leave our precious newborn with a baby-sitter. Even if it's a close friend or grandparents, visions of horrible things happening make it nearly impossible to enjoy ourselves. WHAT IF the baby cries and cries and there's no way to calm her down? WHAT IF she loses her pacifier or gets put on her stomach instead of her side? WHAT IF, God forbid, there's a fire and we never see our child again?

We can "what if" ourselves right back home if we can't let go and trust that our baby will be well taken care of. It goes without saying that no one loves or understands our child as well as we do. But we still have to take an occasional leap of faith and leave him or her in someone else's care. The more we do it, the easier it gets.

Affirmation: I'll only call home once.

Intensity

Q. What's been the toughest thing about being a father?
A. You're afraid to love something so much, you're afraid to be that in love.
　　Bruce Springsteen (Rolling Stone *interview*)

Whenever we open our hearts, we run the risk of having them broken. Never is this more true than in parenting. Our love for our children makes us terribly vulnerable to pain and loss. We can survive other heartbreak, but we'd never recover should anything happen to our children.

Yet the possibility for ecstasy equals the potential for sorrow. Like any passionate love affair, the more we invest of ourselves, the more we stand to lose and gain.

Fortunately for most parents the joy far outweighs the pain.

Affirmation: I never knew I could be so in love.

Sensuality

> *I think when my children are gone I'll have to have beautiful fabrics to wear and sleep and sit on . . . to endure the sensual deprivation of my warm living babies.*
> Nancy Thayer

One tangible trade-off for the hard work of caring for a new baby is the constant sensual pleasure of cuddling, rocking, holding him or her closely against our own skin.

Although my children, now eight and ten, still grant me an occasional hug or cuddle, gone are the days of rocking them for hours, luxuriating in their silky softness, breathing in their warm fragrance.

For now we should appreciate this physical intimacy. Once our children grow older, we find ourselves begging new moms for the privilege of holding their baby. Oh! Just a moment or two to bathe once again in that singular, sensual delight.

Affirmation: Baby, let me hold you.

Mood Swings

She remembered it as a time of intense feeling, the days when their child had just been born.
    Barbara Einzig

All our emotions are amplified in the first days and weeks postpartum. One instant we're filled with the greatest joy we've ever experienced, the next second we're crying for no apparent reason. Both our happiness and sadness are more intense, more vivid, often shifting back and forth faster than we can figure out what's happening.

So what *is* happening?

What's happening is a combination of hormones, fatigue, and the sheer emotional shock of suddenly having a brand-new human being in your care. No wonder you're ecstatic, exhausted, and entirely overwhelmed all at the same time.

Let yourself laugh. Let yourself cry as much as you need to. You're not going crazy, you're simply responding to the powerfully dramatic transition from pregnancy to motherhood.

Affirmation: All my emotions are normal and natural.

Self-discovery

> *If there were no other reasons, this alone would be the value of children: the way they reveal you to yourself.*
> *Elizabeth Berg*

Children are our mirrors. Even brand-new babies reveal our strengths, our weaknesses, our fears as we struggle to live up to our own expectations of motherhood.

It's important to face ourselves honestly ("I see now that I need to develop patience, spontaneity, and work on being more organized"). But it's also important to avoid taking on too much responsibility for our children's happiness ("My baby's crying, and it must be my ineptitude." "If he wasn't in day care, my two-year-old would probably be toilet trained by now").

Some things are realistic yardsticks of our cutting edges. Others have little to do with us. It's important to know which is which.

Affirmation: Motherhood reveals myself to me.

Patience

Everything about a new family takes time.
Judy Blume

And lots of it!

If you were starting a new job, you'd likely give yourself at least a few weeks to get the lay of the land, to understand office politics, to find a routine and a rhythm that's productive and meets your goals.

Yet we expect ourselves to assume the job of motherhood and have everything run smoothly without losing a beat.

This is an incredibly unrealistic expectation! It takes days, sometimes weeks, to learn how to nourish and comfort a newborn. It takes weeks, sometimes months, to figure out how to integrate your existing demands with your new responsibilities. It takes months, sometimes years, to make the complete shift from being a couple to being a family.

Take your time. Gradually everything will fall into place.

Affirmation: I don't have to have it all figured out today.

Honesty

> *The first time I lied to my baby I told him it was his face on the baby food jar.*
>
> Maxine Chernoff

The first time I lied to my baby, I told her she needed a nap because *she* was tired. I caught myself and retracted my statement, instead telling her the real truth: *"You* need a nap because *I'm* tired."

Although little white lies are often convenient, they're rarely the best idea. Especially if we want our children to be honest with us.

Yet sometimes it's hard to know what's a lie and what's misinformation for the sake of prolonging the magic of childhood. Is it better to insist that the Tooth Fairy is real, only to have our six-year-old discover a half-dozen teeth wrapped in toilet paper at the bottom of our sweater drawer? What about Santa Claus? The Easter Bunny? What really happened to the family dog that Tuesday afternoon when he went to the vet and never came back?

Each of us must grapple with the complexities of truth telling, keeping in mind that:

Affirmation: Children are more resilient than we think.

Sacrifice

You learn to give up or postpone many of the pleasures you enjoyed, such as eating when you are hungry, watching a movie all the way through, going to sleep when you are tired.
Lydia Davis

Sacrifice, sacrifice, sacrifice. It's the mantra of motherhood.

Some sacrifices are easier than others. If you're lucky enough to only need five hours sleep, you're probably in relatively good shape. On the other hand, if you're the kind of person who gets dizzy or crabby without three square meals at regular intervals, you may find yourself considering two doughnuts an acceptable lunch.

What's important is to know yourself, know your limits, and make sure you're getting the basics. If sleep is imperative, resist the urge to watch late-night television and go to bed immediately when the baby goes down. If exercise keeps you sane, religiously use your baby-sitter time to work out. If a healthful diet is your priority, be sure there's food in the refrigerator and make time to eat, even if you need to refine your skill with the Crockpot.

Being a good mother means taking good care of your baby. It also means taking good care of yourself.

Affirmation: I'll take good care of myself.

Self–care

> *Every day there is less of me and more of the baby.*
> Carole Itter

Early on it's natural to feel as if your entire identity has been subsumed in motherhood. Every waking hour is spent caring for your newborn. His schedule predominates, his needs prevail, even his baby paraphernalia is slowly taking over the living room.

It's easy to lose yourself unless you make a special effort to do something—at least once a day—just for yourself (and going to work doesn't count). Talk to a friend on the phone. Read a magazine article that interests you. Get a sitter and play tennis, go to a movie, or attend a seminar, anything that helps you recover your sense of self.

Because no matter how devoted you are to your baby, the more fulfilled you are, the more you have to give.

Affirmation: I'll make room for me.

Privacy

I remember moments of peace when for some reason it was possible to go to the bathroom alone.
Adrienne Rich

Who ever thought we'd celebrate the chance to go to the bathroom alone?

But the little things we took for granted assume great value once there's a baby clamoring for our attention. Sleeping past eight o'clock, reading the newspaper, going grocery shopping alone—these become extraordinary luxuries, the subjects of tantalizing daydreams.

Relinquishing our most basic freedoms, then gradually regaining them, makes us fiercely protective of our scarce moments to ourselves. And far more appreciative of them when they come.

Affirmation: I will make the most of these rare moments of peace.

Grandparents

> *You feel completely comfortable entrusting your baby to them for long periods of time, which is why most grandparents flee to Florida at the earliest opportunity.*
> *Dave Barry*

There are grandparents begging to take regular shifts, grandparents on call, and those who say, "I've done my time. Don't expect me to baby-sit."

If grandparents live close by and are eager to care for your baby or even pinch-hit once in a while, count yourself lucky for two reasons: You give your parents the pleasure of getting to know your child. And you get completely comfortable time off knowing your baby is with someone who loves him or her almost as much as you do.

There is, however, a wrinkle. Regardless of how good your relationship is or how respectful they are, grandparents inevitably have their own—probably different—way of doing things. Be assertive about your child-raising beliefs, but careful not to be too heavy-handed or critical. Chances are, even if they stay up later than their bedtime, have to be a little quieter a little more often, or get spoiled with treats, your children will come home none the worse for wear.

Affirmation: I will be tolerant of my children's grandparents.

A Day in the Life

You've just put your eighteen-month-old in day care and you're a wreck. You've called three times, and it's not even noon. How are you supposed to get any work done while worrying whether your child is okay?

Stop calling!

You'll never be totally ready to leave your child; it's natural to miss her and wish you could be there twenty-four hours a day. But once or twice a day, unless your baby is sick, is more than enough times to call your day-care provider. More than that is disturbing and makes it appear you don't trust her, and besides, you'll never get your work done if you're constantly on the phone.

Hard as it is to allow someone else to care for your baby, you must learn to let go. *If* you can't, then it means one of three things: (a) You're not really ready to go back to work, in which case you may need to renegotiate maternity leave; (b) you don't feel confident and secure with your child-care arrangements and may need to reevaluate; or (c) you are simply torn about not being with your child and may want to consider counseling to sort out your feelings.

Affirmation: I'll try to do what's best for my baby and myself, including learning to let go.

Humor

> *As a final bequest I would like to leave my children with a*
> *sense of humor. Living with them has improved mine.*
> Phyllis Theroux

A sharpened sense of humor is one of the side benefits of motherhood. We cultivate it out of necessity; it serves us well in those moments when we don't know whether to laugh or cry.

It's a great advantage to be able to laugh when our six-month-old skips both naps, then finally falls asleep the minute the baby-sitter arrives, when our toddler grins gleefully after emptying our entire sock drawer, when rivers of soapy water drench the kitchen as our two-year-old proudly "does the dishes," resulting in an hour spent cleaning up the damage.

Seeing the comic possibilities keeps things in perspective, the all-important quality that separates mothers who lose it from mothers who can't stop laughing.

Affirmation: I will have a sense of humor about my children.

Setting an Example

Children have never been very good at listening to their elders, but they have never failed to imitate them.
James Baldwin

Too often we are guilty of "do what I say, not what I do." Yet as James Baldwin points out, our children are much more likely to emulate our behavior than follow our words.

Our children are always watching us, aware of our choices, sensitive to the disparity between our actions and our advice. We can't put seatbelts on our two-year-old without fastening our own. We can't insist our four-year-old eat broccoli while we snack on nachos. We can't prod our three-year-old to put his toys away if our own things are in disarray.

If we are to be effective role models, our words and deeds must match. We must do as we say if we expect our children to do the same.

Affirmation: I will set a consistent positive example.

Commitment

I am seeking, I am striving, I am in it with all my heart.
Vincent Van Gogh

We seek the knowledge, the wisdom, the patience to guide our child through every step of the journey.

We strive to be the very best parent we can possibly be, knowing we are still learning, still growing, still stretching to understand what it means to be a mother.

We fully commit to the responsibilities of parenthood. Our love and good intentions are all we need as we continue to try to be the very best mothers we know how to be.

Affirmation: I am in it with all my heart.

Single Moms

Five years ago I thought having children was safe and predictable. Now I think the most courageous thing is to get married and have children, because that seems the most worthwhile.
Candice Bergen

Or, as in the case of Candice Bergen's celebrated TV sitcom character, Murphy Brown, having a baby whether you're married or not.

According to the 1990 census, there are currently over 25 percent single mothers in the United States. For many reasons more women are going it alone, and those who do, deserve support. It's a tough enough job with two parents taking turns; it's an awesome task for any one person to take on alone.

If you're out there raising a child or children by yourself, know that you are to be applauded for your courage, tenacity, and strength.

Affirmation: Single mothers deserve our support.

Nutrition

> *We are allowing a majority of our children to form atrocious dietary habits.*
>
> Dr. Benjamin Spock

There's so much pressure to provide a healthy diet for our children. This is the time when they are building bones, growing teeth, developing the eating habits that will serve them—or sabotage them—the rest of their lives.

Too often, despite our best efforts, we fall short in our nutritional guidelines. Much as the four food groups weigh heavily on our minds, sometimes peanut butter and jelly, microwave ravioli, or a pizza ordered for delivery are simply the best we can do. (Most mothers will even confess to serving an occasional dinner of cereal and toast.)

While it's important—essential, really—to take our children's diet seriously, it's just as important not to pressure ourselves if we can't always manage a protein accompanied by lively green vegetables. Fast food—in moderation—isn't atrocious. As long as we don't make a steady diet of it.

Affirmation: I'll do my best to provide a healthy diet.

Rules

This is not a democracy!
      Anonymous mother

I've known mothers who bark out orders like drill sergeants, and others for whom every extra cookie or extended bedtime is an opportunity for consensus decision making.

Neither is a successful long-term strategy. While "Because I said so," is decisive and effectively closes the debate, it tips the power scales and robs children of their voice and their vote. On the other hand endless negotiation is exhausting and unrealistic; children have neither the reasoning power nor the right to have equal say in every decision.

A balance is needed—and the balance shifts as our children get older. You get to be an autocrat when your baby is under the age of two. From two to five you make executive decisions while sometimes taking their opinions into account. From five on you'd better get ready to defend all your positions. But even then you get to have the final say.

Affirmation: Because I'm the mom.

Teething

> *Adam and Eve had many advantages, but the principal one was that they escaped teething.*
> *Mark Twain*

We feel so helpless watching our baby drool and fret as each new tooth pushes through the surface. As in most other areas of mothering, it's impossible to prevent their pain. All we can do is ease their suffering, knowing it's necessary to their growth.

Meanwhile teething rings, stale bagels, and zwieback crackers help. So does holding and rocking your baby, comforting him any way you can. So does saying to yourself:

Affirmation: These are my child's necessary growing pains.

Inventiveness

Well, another year has gone by and still the Nobel Prize has not yet been awarded to the inventor of the Snugli baby carrier. I can't figure it.
Anna Quindlen

Neither can I.

But whoever came up with this brilliant idea unquestionably deserves some prestigious award, or at least the thanks of mothers everywhere.

They say necessity is the mother of invention. I'd argue that mothers are the inventors of necessary objects, vital to making life with children easier and more manageable.

I'm thankful for the inventors of silent push toys, collapsible strollers, and glow-in-the-dark pacifiers. It's comforting to see myself and mothers everywhere using their creativity to address their children's needs.

Affirmation: I will never underestimate my own inventiveness.

Playfulness

> *Adults are obsolete children.*
> > Dr. Seuss

It's easy to lose our childlike spirit when we are burdened with work, bills, and the other demands of our daily life. Here's one way in which our children are our teachers: Simply being with them awakens the magical creativity that still lies within us.

Reading *The Cat in the Hat* and other beloved Dr. Seuss classics with our children helps us remember how to be spontaneous and playful. So does making up whimsical rhymes, spinning in circles, being silly just for the sake of being silly, and wondering just how many dandelions are populating the front yard.

Playing restores the energy we need to handle all our "adult concerns" with proper perspective and even some delight.

Affirmation: Playing is part of parenting.

Discipline

He that spareth his rod hateth his son.
Old Testament

We all struggle with the issue of discipline: How much? How often? What sort of incentives and punishments best teach our children values, morals, and acceptable behavior?

Most parents rely on time-out (five minutes for young children, a half hour for bigger kids) or reasonable consequences (taking away a toy that's been mistreated or removing a privilege that's been abused).

Although many parents still hit their children as a way to discipline, I personally disagree. While physical punishment certainly gets the message across, we have to question exactly *what* the message is. When we hit our children, even "in their best interest," we are teaching them two things: that we are bigger and more powerful, and that violence is acceptable.

"Tough love" taken to the extreme is never right. Through understanding and patience I can teach my children by my example.

Affirmation: I will learn better ways to discipline my children.

Influence

> *Give me the children until they are seven and anyone may have them afterwards.*
> *Saint Francis Xavier*

Experts in child development generally agree that our child's psyche is most critically shaped between the ages of one and five. After that they're pretty much who they're going to be.

This is an overwhelming thought. That we have so much influence in such a brief period of time. That what we do right now will affect our child for the rest of his life.

It makes us think twice. About the words we use, the way we touch, the choices we make, the lessons and experiences we give our child. Today. Right now. Only at great pains will what we do today ever be undone.

Affirmation: I am shaping my child's future.

Sharing

Conspire with your child.
Daniel Menacker

Our kids are delighted when we confide in them, let them in on secrets, or seek their input in important family decisions. My son, Evan, still talks about the time I took Zoe with me to Florida, and when we returned, he and his father had painted the bathroom a beautiful shade of lavender.

Being on the "inside," whether it's keeping quiet about the surprise party we're planning for Daddy's fortieth birthday or making watercolor signs to welcome Grandma home from a trip, makes children feel important and trusted. It's a way of helping develop their confidence. It's a way of saying:

Affirmation: We're on this team together.

Parenting Styles

> *How to fold a diaper depends on the size of the baby and the size of the diaper.*
> *Dr. Benjamin Spock*

And how to cradle an infant depends on the size of the infant and the size of your arms. And how to discipline a toddler depends on the size of the problem and the size of the toddler. And how to answer a child's question depends on the size of the question and the size of the child.

In fact Dr. Spock's advice is applicable to every stage of parenting. There is no one way to do anything; it all depends on the magnitude of the challenge and the dimensions of the individual child.

Which is both a relief and a challenge. A few guidelines, to be sure. But, on the other hand, no rigid rules other than our own best judgment.

Affirmation: There are many different ways to parent.

Stimulation

In general my children refuse to eat anything that hasn't danced on TV.

Erma Bombeck

My first taste of *Sesame Street* was watching Big Bird sing "Letter B" to the tune of the old Beatles song "Let It Be." I was hooked.

As I look back on those "Thank God it's time for *Sesame Street*" breaks from parenting, I'm still grateful to Ernie, Bert, and the rest of the crew for making learning so much fun.

But, as Erma Bombeck points out, there is a danger that such intense passive stimulation can lead children to tune out when learning isn't quite so entertaining. When Lego blocks don't have legs of their own and must be methodically stacked one on top of the other. When tying shoes is a necessarily repetitive task. When the noodles in chicken soup don't turn cartwheels, sing, or spell our child's name. When they have to learn it the hard way, the old-fashioned way.

Affirmation: Everything in moderation.

Giving In

> *The thing that most impresses me about America is the way parents obey their children.*
> *Edward VIII*

Sometimes we capitulate because we're too tired to argue. We give in just to keep peace, or we give our children way too much power in reaction to having had too little when we were kids.

The irony is the looser we are with our children, the more desperate they are for structure and discipline. They want—and need—us to be in charge. They want—and need—to know what the rules are, *why,* and have consequences spelled out and stuck to.

A year ago my son, Evan, wanted to stay up late. He stared beguilingly into his father's eyes and asked, "How can you say no to me?" His father wisely replied, "Lucky for you I can. Otherwise you'd have to be the parent and I'd have to be the child."

Evan sighed, a mixture of resignation . . . and relief.

Affirmation: My child needs me to be in charge.

Smiles

When you are drawing up your list of life's miracles, you might place near the top of the list the first moment your baby smiles at you.

        Bob Greene

Some say it's gas.

Don't believe it for a minute!

Whatever its origins, it's an amazing moment when your baby's face first lights up in a smile. It's a reward for all the sleepless nights and all the dirty diapers. It feels wonderful to be engaged in such intimate connection, and we can't help smiling back.

This is the first of many miracles to come: the first word. The first step. The first time your child looks you right in the eye and says those incredibly magical words "I love you, Mommy."

Affirmation: What a smile!

Changes

> *Every day you wake up to discover a slightly different person sleeping in that cradle, that crib, that bottom bunk, that dinosaur sleeping bag.*
>
> Joyce Maynard

And each morning we are torn between feelings of excitement over the new person our child is becoming and sadness at how quickly the changes occur.

Watching our children grow is a bittersweet mix of anticipation and loss. As we witness our tiny newborn emerge from his sleepy cocoon, transformed from a sweet, cuddly baby to an active toddler to an inquisitive child, we both celebrate and grieve, thrilled by each new leap, yet painfully aware that time races on.

Not that we would stop it. We welcome our child's growth and strive to savor every moment of every passing day.

Affirmation: I celebrate my child's growth.

A Day in the Life

Every Tuesday you go to a mother-baby group with eight other new moms. Most of the babies are crawling or at least sitting up, while your Emily just rocks on her tummy. And she's one of the oldest! You don't mean to compare her, but you're a little worried that maybe something's wrong.

Relax. Chances are nothing's wrong and Emily is doing just fine.

It's natural to compare our baby's development with others'. Every baby becomes a yardstick for our own; whether the other is an infant or a kindergartner, we worry when our child doesn't appear to keep up.

In reality there is a great range of normalcy in babies' development. Some sit up at four months, while others still need to be propped past their six-month mark. Some babies are early crawlers, others inch along until close to their first birthday, and still others skip it all together and at some point just walk.

It wouldn't hurt to take your child in for a checkup if it will ease your fears. If everything is okay—which it probably is—try to stop worrying. She'll sit up when she's ready, she'll crawl when she's ready; at each step along the way allow her to grow at her own rate, in her own unique way.

Affirmation: What's the rush?

Discovery

He is intoxicated . . . he marvels at the bit of dust he picks up in his hands. . . . A piece of cellophane . . . a scrap of foil . . . a satin ribbon fills him with rapture.
Selma H. Fraiberg

It's amazing to watch our children learn; we can almost see the light click on, the wheels turn inside their heads as more and more begins to make sense to them.

I remember watching Zoe, at six months, open and close a cupboard door, over and over, dozens of times, mesmerized by her amazing discovery. It made me think of that glorious instant when Helen Keller first finger-spelled W-A-T-E-R as she made the now-famous connection between water running over her hand and the meaning of the word.

There are countless opportunities to witness the miracle of learning. When our baby makes the connection between hunger and our breast, when our toddler figures out how to scrunch his way down the steps, when our child begins to decipher the alphabet. We are awed again and again by the joy of discovery and the complexity of the human mind.

Affirmation: What great discoveries my child is making!

Language

When I was born, I was so surprised, I couldn't talk for a year and a half.
                                        Gracie Allen

I once heard of someone who didn't speak a word for the first four years of his life. He was examined by numerous specialists, and no one could figure out what was amiss.

When he was four and a half, his family moved to England. As the airplane landed, he turned to his mother and asked, "Where are we?"

There are many stories of perfectly bright individuals who didn't speak until late; there are kids who talk clearly at nine months and others who babble nonsense syllables until they're two. Every child is different. Again, there is no set time. But when the time comes, it's music to our ears.

Affirmation: My child will speak when he's ready.

Food

> *Spinach. Divide into small piles. Rearrange again into new piles. After five or six maneuvers, sit back and say you're full.*
> Delia Ephron

It's easy to get all wound up over what, when, and how much our children eat. Their nourishment is essential; we'd like to give them a healthy diet and start eating habits that will serve them well the rest of their lives.

While "good mothers" care about what their kids eat, we must be careful not to put too much emphasis on food. Using food as a reward, insisting they swallow spinach when it makes them gag, or pressuring them to finish everything on their plate can backfire and lead to unnecessary power struggles and, in some cases, eating disorders.

Food is one area in which it's important to be picky. About your battles, that is. If it's truly a matter of health, persevere. If not, let them eat cake.

Affirmation: I'll choose my battles.

Responsibility

I'm not your garbage can.
               Anonymous mother

Walking down the street in Berkeley, I overheard a woman say this to her six-year-old son after being handed a dripping ice-cream cone, three bottle caps, and a well-chewed wad of gum.

I laughed out loud, then commiserated with her. Why do our children assume that we're the designated receptacles of their junk? More important, why do we take it from them instead of insisting they take care of it themselves?

This is one of those things that starts early. At first we're thrilled when our baby hands us his half-eaten cracker, but before we know it, we're left holding the bag.

There's a way to nip this in the bud. The next time your child gives you the crusts from his peanut butter sandwich, don't eat them. Don't toss them. Point him in the direction of the garbage can and insist he use it instead of using you.

Affirmation: I deserve respect.

Lightening Up

Here's how to change from being a workman to being a child:
Take off your business suit, sit on the floor, ignore the phone,
and make a fool of yourself.
                                        Zoe Stern

In her book, *Questions Kids Wish They Could Ask Their Parents*, Zoe talks about the value of making time to play with your kids.

Sometimes it's easier said than done. We come home after a long day at work, and by the time we've taken care of dinner, phone calls, and other business, we're way too tired to sit down on the floor and play.

Yet what could possibly be more important? When we take off our business suits, take the phone off the hook, and take time to be with our children—on their terms, even if it's only for a half hour—we give them more than all the videos and toys can buy: We give them our undivided attention.

Affirmation: I'll make time to play with my child.

Diplomacy

Q. *What's the best training for life in politics?*
A. *Motherhood . . . mothers know what to do when there are two kids and one cookie . . . when there are two kids hitting each other, each one claiming the other started it.*

Molly Ivens

All mothers have the qualities of savvy politicians: we're master negotiators, expert peacemakers, totally committed to the concerns of our constituency.

The skills we gain in motherhood are applicable to other parts of life. We become great listeners, able to read between the lines, which enhances our communication in every relationship. We learn to facilitate, moderate, legislate, and govern with care and respect, useful skills in creating a healthy family as well as a peaceful world.

Affirmation: Motherhood is filled with transferrable skills.

Grandparents

> *By some miracle the daughter she complains about (you) gives
> birth to the Perfect Grandchild!*
> *Ellen Sue Stern*

Becoming a mother can be a great source of healing
between us and our own mothers.

For starters we have something wonderful in common
—our baby, who is the light of her life and a positive
reflection on us. No matter what unfinished business remains between us, our mothers can't help but adore our
child and, by association, give us some credit for produc-
ing such a miracle.

This can be a great time to rebuild or cement our
relationship if we're fortunate enough to still have our
mother around. If not, having a child can make us more
appreciative of the woman who gave us the gift of life,
raised us, and helped make us who we are today.

Affirmation: What an opportunity for healing!

Risks

*I love it when people say, "You can't do that." It's like
hearing "I dare you."*
                    Sark

So often we make choices in parenting that are risky,
that go against the grain, that raise the eyebrows of other
parents in our day care or neighborhood.

One woman describes letting her four-year-old make
all her own meals (no cooking); another recalls the time
she encouraged her kids—all under the age of five—to
run around the backyard naked in the middle of a thun-
derstorm. Still another, with tears in her eyes, describes
all the experts, friends, and relatives who cautioned her
against "mainstreaming" her mentally retarded child. She
knew what her son needed, and he thrived.

When it comes to parenting, "you can't do it" is synonymous with "I wouldn't do it" or "I'm afraid of what
will happen if you do it." But even the most well-meaning caution must be weighed against our own deep sense
of what's right for our child. We must dare—even in the
face of criticism—to follow our heart.

Affirmation: I trust my own judgment.

Timing

Keep it simple.

> Anonymous

Common parenting wisdom tells us to keep it simple when answering our young children's questions. Yet too often we overzealously give too much information, making them confused and overwhelmed.

An example: When Zoe was five and Evan was two, a close friend of ours had a baby who was stillborn, which prompted a series of questions on death and dying. As I was tucking them into bed that night, Zoe asked, "If something happened to you and Daddy, where would we go?" Swallowing hard, I answered her, saying, "You'd go to live with Auntie Faith." There was a long pause, then Evan asked, "How would we get there?"

Here I was all ready to explain wills, guardianship, and any number of other details surrounding death, and all that concerned him was who would drive.

Whether our child asks why raindrops fall or where we go after we die, it's important to keep it simple and know that they'll keep asking till they have the answers they need.

Affirmation: I'll follow my child's cues.

A Day in the Life

You've had the most humiliating experience. It was your son's birthday, and the entire family came to dinner at your house. After he blew out the candles, he unwrapped this wonderful Fisher-Price farm from your parents. You were so embarrassed when he threw the box on the floor and burst into tears, saying, "I hate it. Take it back!" You're trying so hard to be a good mother, how can you have raised such a terrible child?

You haven't. You're just doing your arithmetic wrong. A "terrible" child doesn't equal a "bad mother"; in fact there's no such thing as a terrible child, only a child who occasionally does terrible things.

We all take it personally when our child acts out, just as we feel proud when our child is well behaved, courteous, and kind. But we need to separate ourselves from our children and know that their behavior isn't always a direct reflection on our parenting. Most kids act badly at times, and it more likely has to do with being tired, overstimulated, or a normal childhood phase than anything we've done.

Over the years we're likely to feel embarrassed often—when our child hits a playmate, when our toddler breaks the lovely glass vase on our neighbor's coffee table, when our six-year-old talks back to his kindergarten teacher.

We may as well get used to it. And remember, we *are* responsible for helping our children know what's right. We *aren't* responsible for our children's mistakes.

Affirmation: Even the best children sometimes blow it.

Commitment

> *When people ask me what I do, I always say I am a mother first.*
>
> Jacqueline Jackson

We can be a singer, a lawyer, a rocket scientist, but once we have a child, we are always a mother first.

Sometimes this translates into deep conflict; our newborn's under the weather and we must leave him with a brand-new care provider in order to be at work. We're late coming home and only get a half hour before bedtime with our baby. We miss our toddler's first step and have trouble forgiving ourselves, even though it couldn't have been avoided.

Our children are always everpresent in our thoughts. Even when we can't be with them, we carry them near our heart everywhere we go.

Affirmation: I am always a mother.

Trial and Error

If it isn't working, change it.
Vicky Stewart

I heard Vicky say this at a friend's baby shower as each woman there went around the circle and offered her best advice on parenthood. She went on to elaborate: If your baby's crying and you're feeding him, stop. If you're not feeding him, start. If you're standing up, sit down; if you're sitting down, stand up and walk around.

Obvious as it seems, this is sound advice, especially during these first months when your baby can't tell you what's wrong, what he needs, or what would make it right.

Most of the time it's guesswork, trial and error as we gradually learn what works.

Affirmation: Being a mother is a constant experiment.

Support

> *The women of the Samois tribe bring meals to the new mother for the first month following birth.*
> *Folklore*

In many cultures around the world, following birth, mothers and babies are cared for by members of the community. They clean house, massage the new mother, and bring her food so that she can recover and focus her attention on her baby.

Unfortunately in modern urban America most new moms are left virtually alone to cope with the physical and emotional adjustments postpartum. It's natural to feel isolated and depleted with so much to do and so little support.

Since American culture doesn't offer such rituals, it's up to us to create whatever support we can for ourselves, by delivering food, helping with laundry, and any other ways we can lighten new moms' load.

Affirmation: I will ask for—and accept—as much help as possible.

Self-appreciation

I'm searching for my inner child.
                    Anonymous

There's been much written of late on the "inner child." This term usually refers to the living child we once were, which in many cases was wounded and needs to recover self-esteem.

As parents we have great power in forming our child's self-esteem. How we treat our children—whether we respect, listen, and are supportive of their feelings—permanently affects their emotional health.

It is the imperative of each generation to take what we've learned and add it to the stock of wisdom teaching what it takes for children to grow up loving themselves and at peace with the world.

Affirmation: I will help my child to know how lovable she is.

Frustration

> *When the twins turned three, my doctor prescribed Ritalin. I wouldn't dream of giving drugs to my children, but it does help when I take it myself.*
> Lily Tomlin and Jane Wagner

You probably don't need tranquilizers, but there are days when it seems like a handy idea.

The irony is that we can't wait for our children to crawl, and then breathlessly chase after them. We wait for our children to talk, and then wish we had earplugs. We wait for our children to walk, and then they absolutely wear us out.

They don't need tranquilizers. We don't need tranquilizers. *But* if you're really feeling that strung out, it means you need to take a real break. Hire a baby-sitter, ask a friend or grandparent to help out. Do whatever you need to do to calm down and catch your breath.

Affirmation: Take time for a break.

Mistakes

Mistakes are the portals of discovery.
        James Joyce

Every parent makes mistakes. Lots of them. Our new-born screams and screams until we realize the nipple's clogged and he isn't getting any milk. We reprimand our one-year-old for stealing the cookie that in fact her big brother devoured. We forget to send the permission slip for our child's field trip to the zoo.

Mistakes can set off guilt and self-recrimination, *or* we can take them seriously but in stride. Most important, they are lessons. Each time we blow it—and we will—we can discover areas in which we need improvement and make the commitment to try harder. Each time we miss the mark, we can say to ourselves:

Affirmation: I am human. I am learning from my mistakes.

Appreciation

> *We never know the love of our parents for us till we have become parents.*
>
> *Henry Ward Beecher*

Over and over I have heard new parents say that, in having a baby, their appreciation for their own parents has soared.

I remember shortly after Zoe's birth, sitting bleary-eyed in the rocking chair, feeding her at four-thirty A.M. thinking to myself, "Once my mother got up in the middle of the night just like this with me."

In countless ways, having a child makes us aware of the sacrifices our own parents made. As we soothe and nourish and work to provide for our children, we look at their grandparents with newfound gratitude and respect.

Affirmation: Thank you.

Empowerment

Even a two-year-old can be asked whether he wants half a glass of milk or a full glass of milk.
Dr. Haim G. Ginott

In his famous book *Between Parent and Child*, Dr. Haim G. Ginott stresses the importance of giving children choices as a way of cultivating responsibility.

Too often we make choices for our children. Or tell them what to do without inviting their input. Or assume the choices are too trivial to make a difference.

But to a child, being asked is synonymous with being respected. Each time we allow our child to choose—whether it's between milk and juice, a sweater or a jacket, a toy or a story, we empower them, building the confidence to make increasingly big decisions as they grow.

Affirmation: I will encourage my child's input.

Compensation

In the job of home keeping there is no raise from the boss and seldom praise from others to show us that we've hit the mark.
Anne Morrow Lindbergh

The same is true of motherhood.

This is an especially serious problem for moms-at-home, who sometimes face the doubly difficult dilemma of getting no credit for homemaking *or* child raising.

But both moms-at-home and moms-in-the-workplace are sorely lacking in acknowledgment and praise. Our society places little tangible value on child raising; no paycheck, no performance reviews or bonuses, and hardly a word from anyone on what a fabulous job we're doing.

We must all work together to give parenting the value it deserves. Here's one way to start: Each time you notice your mate or another parent doing something well, whether it's taking time to explain something to her child or being especially patient, understanding, or creative, make a point of saying something positive. Do the same for yourself. Keep a journal or a star chart for marking your parenting high points. Reward yourself each time you do something you're especially proud of.

Affirmation: I'm doing a great job!

Exhaustion

No animal is so inexhaustible as an excited infant.
Amy Leslie

Several years ago a study was conducted in which ten Olympic athletes were asked to spend an entire day following after a one-year-old child, doing exactly as he or she did.

Not one of the athletes could keep up. At the end of the day they were flat on their faces, exhausted and panting, desperate for relief.

Whether your baby is six weeks, six months, or a year old, he or she is probably running you ragged. The relentless care of a newborn, the constant surveillance to assure an infant doesn't swallow a penny or a toddler doesn't scramble out of sight, is intensely demanding work.

If you're tired, no wonder! Which is why naps—or at least downtime—are vital. When your baby's resting, rest. Resist the urge to return calls or fold laundry. Take the phone off the hook and rest. It's the only way to survive.

Affirmation: I will rest when the baby goes down.

Improvisation

> *New parents quickly learn that raising children is kind of desperate improvisation.*
> Bill Cosby

The saying "Fake it till you make it" applies beautifully to parenthood.

Especially at the beginning, when we are short on experience, we make up for it by constantly improvising. We try one thing, then another, mixing hearsay with instinct, combining our mother's advice with the latest child-raising books, experimenting until we get it right.

One new mother describes herself as a "research scientist" trying out every possible formula in an effort to find one her baby won't be allergic to. Another discovered quite by accident that the sound of the vacuum was the one thing that would consistently get her baby to sleep. Still another, in a desperate attempt to get some rest, attaches a string to her baby's cradle, which she pulls to rock it during the night when her baby cries.

If there were only two words of advice for new parents, they might be:

Affirmation: Whatever works.

Pressure

In some ways you go through motherhood in an under-siege mentality. You never admit how hard things are till they're safely behind you.

     Liz Rosenberg

In my photo album are pictures of myself with my brand-new baby. I look like a strung-out drug addict. My eyes are glazed with deep, dark circles under them. I'm wearing a soiled T-shirt, clutching a cup of coffee, standing knee-deep in what appears to be a pile of dirty laundry and unopened mail.

In retrospect it's hard to imagine how we survive the ordeals of early motherhood. Sleep deprivation. Colic. Constant uncertainty. The horror that something may happen to our baby.

We look back on these first few weeks and months and are amazed that we got through them in one piece.

But when they're happening, we simply put one foot in front of the other, meeting each challenge with the knowledge that:

Affirmation: Every day life will get easier.

Adoration

The god to whom little boys say their prayers has a face very much like their mother's.
Sir James M. Barrie

Realizing how much power our children give us is both gratifying and overwhelming.

On the one hand it pleases us that our sons and daughters look up to us; on the other hand it's an awesome responsibility knowing that our children expect us to have the wisdom, the judgment, the goodness of God.

Eventually our children learn that we are human and fallible. And it is a good thing. Because there is no living up to our children's image of a deity; it's hard enough to live up to their—and our—image of a good parent.

Affirmation: I needn't be overwhelmed by how much my child looks up to me.

Mother's Day

*Unpleasant questions are being raised about Mother's Day. Is
this day necessary? Isn't it bad public policy?*
Russell Baker

Hardly. But mothers and fathers ought to be honored
every day, not just on official "Hallmark" holidays.

As should children. Sooner or later most kids ask,
"What about Children's Day?" and most parents answer,
"Every day is children's day."

Perhaps every day should also be Parents' Day. Holidays are good reminders to stop and formally honor our
loved ones. But that needn't keep us from making it an
everyday occurrence as well.

Because the times we least expect a hug, a thank-you, a
homemade card with a child's name scrawled on the bottom, often turn out to be the best celebrations of all.

Affirmation: Every day is Mother's Day.

Education

> *One good mother is worth a hundred schoolmasters.*
> George Herbert

We really are our children's first and most influential teachers.

Think about it. Our children learn from us how to walk. How to talk. How to feed themselves and wash themselves and look both ways before crossing the street.

Not to mention the values we teach our children long before they venture out into the world. Saying please and thank you. Sharing. The power of a hug, the importance of cleaning up after themselves, telling the truth, and helping make the world a cleaner, safer place.

Over the years they learn to read. To add and subtract. To solve mind-boggling problems.

Yet no matter how brilliant their teachers are, what they learn from us is the essential foundation for everything that follows.

Affirmation: I teach my child how to love.

Reassurance

Children need love, especially when they don't deserve it.
Harold S. Hubert

When our children disappoint us by acting out, we're apt to withhold our love. We berate or banish. Our angry words or disapproving silence give our child the message that they are unlovable by virtue of having misbehaved.

Children must be reprimanded when they misbehave. However, we must be careful to focus on their actions rather than on their essence, correcting their behavior while reaffirming their innate goodness.

Looking at a child's face when he or she has misbehaved is the best argument for loving discipline. They already feel terrible; their face crumples up in shame and fear at having erred. When this happens, we must be especially loving. We must be sure to convey, I don't like what you did. But no matter what happens:

Affirmation: I will always love you.

Taste

> *I have seen my kid struggle into the kitchen in the morning with outfits that need only one accessory: an empty gin bottle.*
> Erma Bombeck

My daughter, Zoe, calls me the Clothes Police. It is a continual struggle for me to respect her taste and squelch my desire to lay her clothes out at night. (God forbid she wears those torn jeans and someone sees her and thinks they're the only thing in her closet!)

But even little kids want to have a say when it comes to outfitting themselves. Unfortunately their taste and ours rarely mesh. One woman whose taste runs to tailored suits has a one-year-old daughter who's bedazzled by ribbons and bows. Another describes her two-year-old son's favorite outfit as a cross between Liberace and the Little Rascals. My son, Evan, refuses to wear anything other than short-sleeved T-shirts and overalls from Gap Kids.

It's tough to refrain from imposing our tastes upon our kids. But it helps teach us an important lesson: Our children are not a reflection of us. They are individuals with their own (however questionable) style.

Affirmation: I will encourage my child to express his or her own taste.

Expenses

It costs more now to amuse a child than it once did to educate his father.

Vaughn Monroe

The other day I happened to walk into F.A.O. Schwarz at the new MegaMall in Minneapolis. Among the toys were a miniature car that drives, a designer dollhouse, and a stuffed gorilla five feet tall.

Whatever happened to a teddy bear and a forty-nine-cent box of Crayola crayons?

I realize I'm aging myself, but the costs of amusing our children *are* outrageous, far beyond what most of us can—or should have to—afford.

TV, peer pressure, and rampant consumerism all demand we buy in to the idea that our children require lavish toys in order to be entertained. Fact is they don't. As our children get older, the pressure grows to have the newest Nintendo and all the attendant paraphernalia. We have the choice—and the responsibility—to resist going overboard. More often than we realize, the old-fashioned toys—a yo-yo, deck of cards, pickup sticks, and Slinkies—can still amuse our children. And keep us out of debt.

Affirmation: Keep it simple.

Going Out

> *A baby-sitter is a teenager who comes in to act like an adult while the adults go out and act like teenagers.*
> *Harry Marsh*

Go ahead!!! It can be hard to leave our babies with sitters, especially teenagers. What if they tune out the baby while they're talking on the phone . . . or forget to feed her . . . or forage through our closet . . . or invite their friends over for a wild party . . . or . . . ?

Meanwhile how can we possibly enjoy ourselves? We may as well just stay home.

Wrong! It's important—vital—to make time to get out, away from the baby, even for a few hours. The time we spend on a romantic date with our mate, having dinner with a friend, going for a walk, or even wandering around a store reenergizes and refreshes us. It makes us better parents. It reminds us that we still have a life!

Affirmation: I deserve an occasional night out.

Skill Building

Parenthood remains the greatest single preserve of the amateur.
Alvin Toffler

What other full-time endeavor in the world has no job description, no formal training, no prerequisite other than desire?

Yet what more does anybody really need? We are all amateurs in the beginning. By the time our child is out of diapers, we could lead training seminars.

Here time and experience are the only teachers. We try our best, make mistakes, learn from them, and improve as we go.

It's the one way—the only way—to become a professional parent.

Affirmation: We're all amateurs.

A Day in the Life

Your wife says she wants you to be an equal parent, but every time you try, she takes the baby out of your arms. She criticizes how you burp her, she makes fun of how you diaper her. You're starting to feel like you can't do anything right.

Of course you do! How else could you feel when all your efforts are criticized and dismissed?

You don't say whether your wife is at home with the baby, but if she is, this may be one reason why she's so overprotective. It's natural for some moms-at-home to have trouble detaching from their baby enough to let fathers take their rightful turn.

Your desire to coparent is admirable; however, this situation requires compromise on both your parts. Your wife needs to let go a little and make a lot more room for you to parent in your own way. And you need to be open to her feedback and suggestions, as long as they're respectful and in your baby's best interests.

Affirmation: I'll share the responsibility of parenting.

Patience

Never play peek-a-boo with a child on a long plane trip. There's no end to the game. Finally I grabbed him by the bib and said, "Look, it's always gonna be me!"
        Rita Rudner

No matter how hard we try always to act like the "designated adult," there are times we simply run out of patience. We blow our cool. We lose our composure and forget to give the "parentally correct" response that will foster our child's self-esteem and prevent years of therapy down the road.

Sometimes we even stomp our feet or throw tantrums, acting more like our two-year-old than our two-year-old. At these times it's best to take a deep breath, a short time-out, have a good laugh at ourselves, and start over.

Affirmation: Peek-a-boo!

Humility

> *Never give in. Never, never, never, never.*
> *Winston Churchill*

Terrible advice for parents!

Knowing when to stand firm in our decisions and when to give in to our children is a constant challenge and part of what makes for good, responsible parenting.

While we want our children to respect our authority, we must also be open to their input and willing genuinely to consider their point of view. If they're right (which they sometimes are!), we must swallow our pride and reevaluate our position. If, however, they're simply pushing the limits, we must have the wherewithal to stand our ground.

Both are necessary. Both require humility and wisdom.

Affirmation: I'm willing to listen.

Messes

One of the most important things to remember about infant care is: Never change diapers in midstream.
Don Marquis

Which there's no way to check in advance.

Face it. There isn't a parent anywhere who hasn't been spit on, peed on, showered with half-digested food.

Although we know we can count on being in the line of fire, we can't predict when the attack will come. (It's usually right after we've changed into our best clothes ready to walk out the door to a special event.)

Babies are messy, which is why most new moms live in their oldest, most well-worn sweatshirts. Consider it an occupational hazard. Save it as a "war story" to laugh about with the perpetrator when he or she grows up.

Affirmation: I will expect to get dirty.

Ambition

> *Your responsibility as a parent is not as great as you might imagine. You need not supply the world with the next conqueror of disease or major motion picture star.*
> Fran Lebowitz

What parent hasn't fantasized their child writing the great American novel? Winning the Olympic Gold Medal? Discovering a cure for cancer?

Although we all insist we simply want our kids to be healthy and happy (which of course we do!) the truth is, we often wish for much more.

It's essential to identify our children's gifts and nurture their special talents. But it's wrong to expect them to fulfill our ambitions.

They must fulfill their own dreams. And we must love and encourage them, whatever those turn out to be.

Affirmation: My child has the right to his or her own ambitions.

Silliness

Getting down on all fours and imitating a rhinoceros stops babies from crying.
P. J. Rourke

Parents stop at nothing!

Especially when it comes to turning our children's sobbing to smiles.

But even when our antics aren't prompted by the frantic need to distract or console, parenting regularly includes making a fool of ourselves.

Inhibitions disappear as we make moo-moo sounds, wiggle our ears, and crawl on all fours just to get a laugh.

And lucky for us. Because these are some of the best moments of motherhood.

Affirmation: I'm willing to make a fool of myself.

Casualness

> *God knows that a mother needs fortitude and courage and tolerance . . . but I praise casualness.*
> *Phyllis McGinley*

Casualness! A quality rarely mentioned in connection with motherhood, yet truly among the fundamental tools of the trade.

Witness, for example, a seasoned mother's reaction to her eight-month-old baby toppling off a kitchen stool. She calmly reaches to retrieve him, and in her most even voice asks, "Are you all right, honey?" all the while checking for bruises and bumps. The baby takes his cue from her and soon happily resumes playing.

Cultivating casualness has long-term benefits: The slightest arch of the eyebrow prevents our two-year-old from filching a cookie; the understated "Aren't you a little late?" when our teenager comes home after curfew keeps panic under control and punishment in perspective.

Here's the key: The less we overreact, the more power our words and actions have when we *really* need to make an impact.

Affirmation: I'll keep my cool.

Affection

The best sex education for kids is when Daddy pats Mommy on the fanny when he comes home from work.
Dr. William H. Masters

I know. The blatant sexism in this quote is appalling. And from one of the most enlightened sex educators of our time!

So let's update the scenario to read something like: "The best sex education for kids is when parents hug and kiss each other after they *both* finish work." Now we can more easily see the wisdom in his words.

It's hard to keep romance alive, especially during the early weeks following birth. But physical affection is vital for two reasons: Touching and being touched are restorative and replenishing. And whether or not they understand it, seeing our love for each other helps our children feel loved and secure.

Affirmation: Want a hug?

Home

Bumper sticker:
AUNTIE EM: HATE YOU,
HATE KANSAS, TAKING DOG.
DOROTHY

There's no place like home, which is why what we're doing with and for our children is so vitally important: creating a sanctuary to which they will always gladly return.

Yet there are times they'll threaten to run away. Or wish they had other parents. Or lived in another house in another neighborhood.

If we allow our children to pack their proverbial suitcase occasionally and fantasize the freedom to leave, we also give them the freedom to find their way home again.

Affirmation: I'm making a home for my family.

Problems

No one can say of his house, "There is no trouble here."
Oriental proverb

We hope and pray that our family will be the exception to the rule, that we will magically escape the trauma of illness, financial woes, divorce, and all the other troubles that threaten our happiness and security.

Yet we know life brings pain. No matter how vigilant we are, we will inevitably face hard times, times when we say to ourselves, *This* can't *be happening in* our *family.*

The truth is, it isn't the troubles we go through but how we weather them that makes us a healthy family and a safe haven. Troubles will come, that we can't control. What we *can* control is how, as a family, we meet these challenges. If we talk about them, allow our children to express their pain, fear, and disappointment and know they will survive, we give them necessary tools that will serve them long after childhood troubles have passed.

Affirmation: I can't prevent my children's pain, but I can ease their way.

A Day in the Life

You really want your parents to take care of your nine-month-old daughter, but there's lots of things they do that make you uncomfortable. Like pushing her to eat. And letting her cry herself to sleep. And pretending to be sad when she doesn't want to be kissed and hugged. You don't want to get into it with your parents. But you don't want them to screw up your child either. How can you express your concerns without starting a fight?

Many new parents find themselves in this bind. We're committed to fostering a close relationship between our parents and their grandchild, yet we wince at their antiquated child-rearing techniques.

It's especially frustrating when we see our parents repeating the mistakes we feel they made with us. The difference is now we can stand up for ourselves. And we have the right and the obligation to protect our children.

In doing so, we must be careful not to reenact our own battles and instead focus on positive strategies for bridging the generation gap. A good start is to give grandparents the benefit of the doubt and assume they have only the best intentions. Second, we must attempt to be assertive —not aggressive—in expressing our preferences. Finally it's important to choose our battles. If it's something critical, find the courage to broach the subject. If not, let it go.

Affirmation: I'm willing to give my parents the benefit of the doubt.

Compassion

Having family responsibilities and concerns just has to make you a more understanding person.
        Sandra Day O'Conner

Parenting has a deeply humanizing effect. We become kinder, more empathetic, more compassionate. We learn to set our own needs aside and put another person's first. Knowing the fierce love we feel for our child, it's impossible to ignore the horrifying images of sick and hungry children halfway across the world. Our hearts go out to their mothers; we feel their pain.

Which isn't to say that parenting is the only way to "grow a heart." But it's a darn good way. As we tuck our own children safely into their beds, we say a prayer of gratitude for their safety and well-being.

Affirmation: Being a mother makes me more compassionate.

Manners

> *It is not a bad thing that children should occasionally, and politely, put parents in their place.*
> Colette

This is one of my favorite parts of parenting: If we're willing, we get the benefit of our children's wisdom.

Not always easy medicine to swallow. It's embarrassing to heed our children's admonishments and own up to our mistakes. When they scold us for swearing, ask why we told that white lie, or confront us for not wearing our seatbelts, we feel caught in the act and weakened in our authority.

In fact we are strengthened by our ability to hear what they have to say. Because it takes great courage to be honest with our children and with ourselves about our failings. In doing so, we strive to improve. And we give our children the message that just as we aren't perfect, they needn't be either.

Affirmation: I don't always have to be right.

Delegating

I'm going to stop punishing my children by saying, "Never mind! I'll do it myself."
                    Erma Bombeck

Yes!!!

While it's the path of least resistance, eliminates arguing, and gets the job done, there's a heavy price!

When we "punish" our children by giving up and doing it ourselves, we really punish ourselves. We end up doing three times as much. And they don't learn to take responsibility for themselves.

Everyone loses.

In the short run it's easier. In the long run we do a great disservice to ourselves and our children. The better path is to push through and say, "Do it *yourself.* And let me know when it's finished."

Affirmation: I won't do for my children what they can do for themselves.

Threats

> *Just wait until your father comes home!*
> *Countless mothers*

Many of us heard this refrain as we were growing up. It was an ominous threat and an unhealthy setup for two reasons: (a) Mothers abdicated responsibility for providing discipline; (b) fathers got set up as the "bad guy" responsible for punishment. The result: We were scared of our fathers and didn't take our mothers very seriously.

None of which promotes healthy families.

Personally I'm hoping these words disappear from our repertoire. Because as mothers and fathers move toward equality, we must be sure to share both the tender and the tough parts of parenting. Anything less deprives us all.

Affirmation: The buck stops here.

Martyrdom

A mother is a person who, seeing there are only four pieces of pie for five people, promptly announces she never did care for pie.

Tenneva Jordan

All too often motherhood turns into martyrdom.

Although sacrifice is admirable, there's a limit to how far we should go. If we never forgo our own pleasure to further our family's, we are selfish. But if we consistently subjugate our own needs and desires, we end up resentful and angry. And the more we do it, the more we're taken advantage of.

A balance is best. Our children admire our generosity and selflessness. They also respect us when we respect ourselves.

Affirmation: I count.

"Difficult Kids"

Likely as not, the child you can do least with will do the most to make you proud.
Mignon McLaughlin

In recent years a slew of books on raising "difficult children" have hit the bookstores.

There are kids with serious behavior disorders that clearly require professional attention. But there are lots of children who are simply strong, willful, and demanding individuals.

You know if you have one. Your baby isn't docile; he sleeps restlessly and requires lots of attention. Your one-year-old is constantly on the go and into everything. Your two-year-old constantly asks why—and doesn't accept your explanations.

This makes parenting harder. It tests patience and requires greater ingenuity. But it doesn't mean there's anything wrong—you simply have a more challenging child.

Affirmation: I'm up to the challenge.

Pushing

We're not going to push them . . . but Pam and Edie are already giving Ivan violin lessons and they're signing him up for a Tiny Tot Transformation Seminar.
      Lily Tomlin and Jane Wagner

Years ago I met a woman in a parent-child group whose four-year-old son was an alumnus of the Better Baby Institute.

Frankly he didn't seem any better off than the rest of the children in the class; if anything, he appeared pressured and anxious, especially when he was expected to perform.

Why must we push our children? So they can do us proud? So they can enter college at fifteen? Is it really healthy to encourage our babies to walk before they're ready and read before they've entered kindergarten?

It's natural to want our children to achieve. To keep up with the rest of the kids on the block. But it's best to let them grow and blossom at their own pace.

Affirmation: Everything in its own time.

Joy

Say the word "daughter" slowly . . . notice the way it lingers on the tongue like a piece of candy.
Paul Engle

Right now, this very moment, close your eyes and think about your son or daughter. Take an interlude from washing undershirts, changing diapers, making dinner, to savor all your pleasure in becoming a mother. Picture your baby's perfect skin, feel the sensual delight of cradling him or her in your arms, recall the moment of birth and all the tenderness you feel for your child.

Now, slowly, say to yourself, *This is my son*. Or, *This is my daughter*. Notice how the words fill you with pride. And pleasure. And joy.

Affirmation: It's so sweet.

Growing Up

It will be years before you know it. The fingerprints on the wall appear higher and higher. Then suddenly they disappear.
Dorothy Euslin

When my children were tiny, I remember everyone saying, "The time goes so fast. Before you turn around, they're all grown." Back then it was hard to imagine that the baby would be big enough to stand up in her crib, the one-year-old tall enough to open the cupboard, the two-year-old dextrous enough to pull on his coat.

Yet those days do come, and sooner than we expect. At first we anxiously await our children's every move forward, measuring their growth by inches and pounds. Later we mark time by their significant milestones: their first step, first word, the first time they draw a picture or make a friend.

Keep a record of all of it. Create scrapbooks and videos. Measure their growth with a chart on the bedroom wall.

Most of all, notice everything. The expressions on your child's face. What he or she says and feels. How *you* feel as you watch the fingerprints on the wall get higher and higher and then suddenly fade away.

Affirmation: I'll notice every moment.

Anger

> *When angry, count to four; when very angry, swear.*
> Mark Twain

We enter into parenting terrified of losing our temper; God forbid we should scream or swear and cause horrible, irrevocable harm to our child.

Yet even the best, most patient and even-tempered parents get angry at their kids. It's human. It's natural. It's only a problem when there's a consistent pattern of screaming or, just as damaging, putting the lid on so tight, we eventually explode.

Counting to four—or maybe even twenty-four—is good advice. But sometimes we still need to let our anger out. There's no harm done, as long as we own it, saying, "I'm angry," not "You're bad." As long as we aren't abusive or out of control. And as long as, once we do it, we say "I'm sorry," and mean it.

Affirmation: I'm sorry.

Flexibility

If there's a pitch you keep swinging at and keep missing, stop swinging at it.

Yogi Berra

You're determined to nurse until your baby weans herself, but running home at lunch and having a breast pump at work is running you ragged.

You're dead set against imposing schedules, but the baby is up and down every fifteen minutes.

You're opposed to playpens—having read frightening consumer reports—but you can't be glued to the baby every waking hour.

In other words, you're striking out!

Here's some coaching from World Series Champion Mothers: Switch-hit. Try a change-up. Give yourself a break.

Your commitments are admirable as long as they up your "batting average." When they aren't getting you on base, it's time to rethink your approach.

Affirmation: I'm open to suggestions.

Power

> *One of the first lessons a president has to learn is that every word he says weighs a ton.*
> *Calvin Coolidge*

The same is true of mothers.

They overhear us talking about someday going to Disneyland, and they're packing their Mickey Mouse ears. We threaten to send their uneaten dinner to Africa, and they hand us a postage stamp. We casually mention the possibility of snow, and the next thing we know, they're out the door with their boots on.

Kids take everything literally. When my friend Lauren's son, Malcolm, was seven, he was sick with the flu. She took his temperature. For the next two hours he followed her around the house crying. Finally she discovered what was wrong: "I want my temperature back!" Malcolm plaintively wailed.

We have to watch what we say. Knowing our children are listening—and taking our words to heart.

Affirmation: I'll watch what I say.

Faith

My children have a Higher Power and it's not me.
Carolyn White

Thank God!! Or, whoever or whatever your Higher Power is.

It's a great relief to remember there is a limit to our influence over our children's lives. Although we have mighty powers to create, protect, nurture, and guide, we don't have ultimate control over their destiny. Just as our own lives are subject to forces we can't always understand, so are our children's.

It is our task to guide them in their spiritual path. Beyond that we can only pray for their happiness and safety.

Affirmation: My child's life is unfolding according to plan.

Idealization

> *Lovers, children, heroes, none of them do we fantasize as extravagantly as we fantasize our parents.*
> Francine du Plessix Gray

Parents are larger than life; our children see us as superheroes, capable of bionic feats and heroic achievements.

Which is to say, their picture of us is a little out of focus. At a booksigning for one of my books, my son, Evan, once asked if I was as famous as Michael Jackson. My own mother says that for years I imagined her much wealthier than she was (I distinctly recall once telling my third-grade friends that I lived in a small castle).

It's flattering to be idealized; but it has its downside: When our children figure out we're simply human beings, not mythic figures, they're bound to be disillusioned.

Better to be real right now, displaying our shortcomings as readily as our virtues. It's a little less dazzling, but less disappointing in the long run.

Affirmation: I'll let my child see the real me.

Depression

Noble deeds and hot baths are the best cures for depression.
Dodie Smith

Postpartum depression, mother's blues, exhaustion, boredom, anxiety, and profound feelings of isolation are all *normal* responses in the early months of motherhood.

If you're experiencing *some* of these feelings *some* of the time, there's no cause for concern. If, however, you're experiencing *many* of these feelings *most* of the time, you may need professional care and support.

Assuming you're in the "Sometimes" category, then do heed the above advice: Noble deeds and hot baths *are* terrific antidotes. Most likely you've got the noble-deeds part down; constant sacrifice and giving are the norm for new moms.

Hot baths, on the other hand, require real attention to self-care. Make a commitment to nurture yourself—on a daily basis—with nourishing food, loving friends, and as much rest and relaxation as you can manage.

Affirmation: There are ways to lift my spirits.

Family Jokes

> *Family jokes, though rightly cursed by strangers, are the bond that keeps most families intact.*
> *Stella Benson*

The first time I shared Thanksgiving dinner with my ex-husband, David's, family, I felt utterly left out in the cold. It wasn't that they weren't friendly or warm or welcoming. It was the family jokes. I didn't get them. I didn't think they were funny. Gales of laughter over some shared memory of Thanksgiving past when his mother forgot to put the marshmallows on the sweet potatoes left me wondering if I'd married into a clan of lunatics.

Now that I am a mother, I understand the importance of family jokes. Children delight in them; and humor is a way of bridging generations.

So make a point to remember the funny little things that happen and tell and retell them to your child—especially when he or she is star of the story. When your seven-year-old proudly tells "the tale of the falling-down diaper," your own laughter will tell you how deeply bonded your family really is.

Affirmation: You had to be there.

Sanctuary

I know now how I could feel homesick at home.
G. K. Chesterton

At first glance this quote makes me sad. To be home-sick at home seems like a family that's failed.

Unfortunately many of us felt this way growing up. I know plenty of people who still dread returning home for the holidays, fearful of once again feeling alienated in the one place where we "should" feel the greatest sense of belonging.

It doesn't have to be this way. And therein lies the hope. Our home—the one we are building right now—can and should be a safe haven where our children are free to be themselves. A warm, friendly port where we turn for comfort amid life's storms.

Let us pledge to make our families a place where every member can always feel at home.

Affirmation: Our home is a sanctuary.

Dependency

> *Children are dependent and needy by nature, not by choice.*
> John Bradshaw

At times we resent how much our children ask of us. We feel burdened by their absolute dependency; their constant need for care.

When we feel this way, it's important to remember that, as Bradshaw, an expert on family systems, says, children can't help being needy. It's just the way it is.

Which doesn't eliminate our occasional anger and frustration. Just because something is natural doesn't mean we have to like it. Here's one thing that makes acceptance easier: Make sure your own needs are met. When we ignore our own nature, we end up resentful. When we take good care of ourselves—in whatever way is meaningful to us—we're better able to accept and meet the needs of our children.

Affirmation: Little by little my child will become increasingly independent.

Individuation

I started the process of learning to treat my daughter as a separate person with an identity of her own.
Margaret Mead

This is a lifelong process all parents struggle with.

We want our children to be independent individuals separate from ourselves. On the other hand we can't help but project our own expectations, hopes, and dreams in their direction.

We don't always know when we're doing it. We celebrate our one-year-old's determination, yet wish she'd be a little easier going like her dad. We steer our two-year-old away from ruffly dresses and toward miniature replicas of our T-shirts and jeans. We tell our three-year-old he can be anything he wants when he grows up, yet secretly hope he'll follow in our footsteps.

Maybe he will. Maybe he won't. Real love requires us to encourage our children to be themselves—who *they* are, not who *we* want them to be.

Affirmation: I honor my child's individuality.

A Day in the Life

You've been up since five A.M. feeding the baby and rushing her to day care in time to make your seven o'clock meeting with your boss. He's offered you a promotion; it will mean working harder, later, and coming in on weekends. You're torn. Freaked out. Guilty and confused. Have you turned into one of those women people accuse of letting other people raise their child? If you want a career so badly, maybe you shouldn't have had a baby. . . .

STOP IT!

Stop beating yourself up for attempting the challenge of a lifetime: to be a good—no, *great*—mother and to succeed in your career. This is tough enough without making yourself feel guilty.

Still, it *is* confusing to try to blend family and career. Here's your "out-in-the-workplace-mom" emotional survival kit:

1. Child care you feel absolutely secure with.
2. Help from your partner (if you have one).
3. A new contract with your employer spelling out the terms (commitments *and* limits) of your responsibilities.
4. A moms-in-the-workplace support group.
5. TIME. This *will* get easier. Especially if every single day you repeat to yourself:

Affirmation: I am providing for my child in every possible way.

Nursing

Are you hungry? I have bagels and breast milk.
  Hope Steadman (thirtysomething)

With these words Hope, holding her brand-new baby,
Leo, greets her mother-in-law, who's arrived in town for
the bris.

What struck me about this scene was Hope's combination of humor and irony, with a sprinkle of self-depreca-
tion thrown in. She adds, "You're all here, and all I can
do is lactate," which made me want to break the television screen, shake her by the shoulders, and scream,
"Hope, Hope, stop apologizing. What could be more
important than lactating!?!"

If you feel like a milk machine, if your life has been
reduced to a steady diet of lactating, nursing, expressing,
and lactating again, you're not alone. Nursing is repetitive. At times painful. Certainly not very glamorous.

But remember this: You are making a dramatic contribution to your child's future.

**Affirmation: I won't downplay the importance of
what I'm doing.**

Busyness

> *Having children doesn't turn us into parents. It just makes us busy.*
>
> *Polly Berrien Berrends*

Remember your fantasies of motherhood? Sitting by the window rocking your baby in your arms. Playing in the park, reading fairy tales. Long, cozy talks in the late afternoons sharing secret wishes and dreams.

Now you know the harsh truth. Much of the time parenting is more about chaos than coziness. Mothering is slipped in amid the racket and the running that consume our everyday lives.

Yet in spite of—or perhaps because of—all the clatter and clutter, we *do* become mothers. It happens along the way. The hugs and kisses we give as they're dashing out the door; the advice dispensed while we're washing dishes; the heart-to-heart talks while they're soaking in the bathtub—it is these moments, collected and distilled, that make us into our children's mothers.

Affirmation: I'll find the moments in the mayhem.

Fear

Perfect love casteth out fear.
                    John 4:18

Parental love is the most perfect love there is. Our capacity for affection, devotion, and passionate protectiveness reaches far beyond any other relationship we've ever had or ever will.

And our fear is in direct proportion to our love. The intensity of our feelings for our children makes the idea of anything happening to them utterly unspeakable—beyond our worst nightmare.

How do we live with such overwhelming fear? The answer lies in our love. Perfect love is unconditional—we love our children no matter what, standing by them in moments of darkness. Perfect love is trusting—we count on their resiliency and trust our own ability to help them when in need. And perfect love is powerful—we have the faith and courage to love them in the face of our fear.

Affirmation: My love is greater than my fear.

Graciousness

The perfect relationship between parent and child is as host and guest.

Evelyn Waugh

Think about it.

How does a gracious hostess act?

Warm, interested, sensitive, and eager to make her guests feel comfortable and at home.

And how does a guest act—the sort you'd want to invite back?

Considerate, appreciative, unassuming, and ready to help clear the table without being asked.

Not a bad model for parents and children. If we treat each other with the care we extend to a host or guest, we might all enjoy ourselves a lot more.

Affirmation: Let's make it a party.

Creativity

Another thing that seems quite helpful to the creative process is having babies.

Faye Weldon

Giving and nurturing life releases a wellspring of creativity. We find ourselves itching to express ourselves by writing poetry, playing the piano, taking that watercolor class we've always wanted to try.

The problem is finding the time. And making the commitment to release the artist in ourselves without compromising the other competing demands in our lives.

There's only one way to do it and that's to do it. Let your creativity loose by setting aside fifteen minutes a day to draw in a sketch book or scribble in your journal. If that seems like too much, plan one day a month to check out the latest art exhibit, or attend a concert where all you have to do is sit back, close your eyes, and let the music fill your soul.

Affirmation: I'll nurture the artist in myself.

Support

> *Moms' Support Group:*
> *How do you make time?*
> *Oh, we just call each other on the phone and whine about*
> *how we don't have time to get together.*
> Cathy *comic*

When my friend Jan's baby was born, she was desperate to find part-time day care. "Just put a notice up at schools or the grocery store," I kept encouraging her. It took her almost three months to follow my advice. Why? She had a baby. The last thing she had time for was running around town trying to get the help she needed so she'd have the time to find the help she needed.

You see the dilemma. In these early weeks and months even the littlest things that could help make life easier—arranging child care, getting together with other moms and babies, even making a haircut appointment that could give you a lift—take more time and energy than we can muster.

Make the time. Find the energy.

It's well worth it to make those field trips into the real world. They are small investments with huge returns.

Affirmation: I'm willing to make an investment in myself.

Appreciation

Just the other morning I caught myself looking at my children for the pure pleasure of it.
Phyllis Theroux

We spend hours staring at our children. Looking at them worriedly, praying as they hurtle skyward on the swing set. We scrutinize them critically, wishing their hair was curlier, their disposition was sweeter, that they'd crawl already like the other babies on the block.

So how about just sitting back and enjoying the view? There's nothing more breathtaking than seeing our baby or child through unworried, uncritical, unconditionally loving eyes. Take a moment to look. Notice how fabulous your child really is. How beautiful. How competent. How amazing and unique. Gaze at your child for the pure pleasure of it.

Affirmation: Baby, I see you.

Roots

> *We are always in the process of designing our descendants.*
> Willard Gaylin

Consider the power and mystique our ancestors hold over us. Grandma Becky, who came over on the boat. Great-uncle Wilbert, who ran the five-and-dime during the Depression. Aunt Mary, who had eleven children and actively fought for the right to vote.

Someday we will be framed photographs on our children's mantels, the stuff of family folklore, the stories they pass on to their own children.

These are our descendants. We will be their ancestors. Together:

Affirmation: We are history in the making.

Guilt

There is no contradiction between being a good mother and leaving a child in the care of another adult for part of each day.

Sirgay Sanger, M.D., and John Kelly

It's hard to believe—really believe—that there's no conflict between being a good mother and leaving our child in day care.

The struggle rages on within ourselves. It's the critical inner voice that says, "Good mothers take care of their children all the time." It's the frightened inner voice that says, "If I'm not with my children, will they be okay?" It's the defensive inner voice that says, "I *have* to work. It's not like I have a choice!"

We can—and must—silence these voices. They're destructive and they're false. Instead say to yourself:

Affirmation: I am a good mother. My children are fine. I'm caring for my child in many wonderful ways.

A Day in the Life

You've finally gotten it together to go out for dinner. Your baby's sitting in the infant seat on the table; an acquaintance passes by, stops, and says to you, "How's the baby?" Then he turns to your husband and asks, "How's your job?" Why do you feel like throwing the platter of rigatoni in his face?

Because you're mad—and for good reason. You have a full-time job. And your husband has a full-time baby. Your friend's seemingly innocent yet obviously sexist comment diminishes both you and your husband and fails to acknowledge how each of your lives has changed as a result of parenthood.

Here's where education comes in. You needn't whip out your briefcase and your husband needn't whip out a diaper and demonstrate his technique right there in the restaurant. Instead simply smile. "Our baby's fine. And so are *both* of our careers. Thanks for asking."

Affirmation: It's important to speak up for myself.

Memories

All grown-ups were once children, although few of them remember it.

Antoine de Saint-Exupéry

Stop for a moment and recall your earliest childhood memories. Conjure up the world through a child's eyes—your own. Remember the crackling sounds of leaves beneath your feet, the towering Christmas tree covered with lights, the sweet smell of your mother's perfume as she tucked you into bed. Remember, too, what scared you, what worried you, what you desperately wanted to be reassured about.

All these memories are accessible; it helps to recall them, especially at those moments when we're tired of being an adult or when we're unsure how best to respond to our children.

Then it's good to remember we, too, were children once. Not so very long ago.

Affirmation: I remember.

Vulnerability

> *I tried never to let my kids ever see me cry.*
> Carol Burnett

That makes *me* want to cry!

We do ourselves and our children a disservice when we hide our sorrows and muffle our tears behind a cheery facade. We don't get to express and release our full range of feelings, *and* our children learn to cover their own sadness as well.

We can all learn from Carol Burnett's rueful revelation. Perhaps one of the world's greatest comediennes would have been better off removing her "clown face" once the curtain fell. It helps children to see their mother as a real person, sometimes happy, sometimes sad.

Affirmation: It's important to let my children see my real emotions.

Acknowledgment

All day I did the little things, the little things that do not show.

Blanche Ban Kudee

"What did you do today?" I ask my friend Maggie, mother of Abe, age ten; Sophie, age seven; and Eliana, age three.

"Not much," Maggie replies. "I made pancakes for breakfast, darned socks, designed two Halloween costumes, drove Abe to piano lessons, grocery-shopped, took Sophie to the pediatrician, vacuumed, planted bulbs in the garden, made egg rolls for dinner, and read five books to Elly."

Oh, that's all.

"It's so easy to dismiss all the little things—the incredibly important little things—that make up a mother's day. To act as if they're nothing—and consequently that our time isn't valuable or well spent.

Try this experiment: At the end of this week write down everything you've accomplished as a mom. Include *everything*. Now look at your list and ask yourself this question: How big a difference am I making in my family's life?

Affirmation: A huge difference!

Challenges

> *I was devastated by the news of my daughter's deafness, but determined to help her learn and grow strong and lead as normal a life as possible.*
>
> Beverly Sills

What an ironic twist of fate for world-famous opera singer Beverly Sills to be faced with the challenge of accepting her daughter's deafness.

If you are the parent of a special-needs child, then you deserve enormous support for the difficulties you face.

Although most children don't have dramatic disabilities, many have problems in one area or another, whether physically or psychologically; whether it's bed-wetting, allergies, or having trouble making friends.

As parents it hurts to see our children struggle. We worry about their being accepted. We worry about their happiness and emotional health. We want them to succeed, and we know we can only protect them so much.

It is only by letting go and letting them take on difficulties that they grow strong and learn what they can do. In their moments of mastery—and in their moments of defeat—we learn what it really means to be a parent.

Affirmation: Every child is special.

Adoption

Some people make work their personal life, but I chose to have a family. That's my career.
Mia Farrow

Mia Farrow, as much as anyone in recent history, has redefined our definition of family by raising three biological children along with seven adoptive children, including one child who is blind, one with cerebral palsy, and others with developmental difficulties stemming from malnutrition and neglect.

It takes great courage and commitment to raise a biological child. It takes a little bit extra to offer energy, comfort, and financial and emotional security to one of the millions of children in this world desperately in need of a home.

If you are an adoptive parent, know the value of the very special gift you are giving—the gift of a safe and secure future to a child for whom the word *mother* has a very special meaning.

Affirmation: Being an adoptive mother is an extra blessing.

Crawling

> *For the first six months or so, your opponent has been unable*
> *to escape. Alas, the rules are about to change drastically.*
> *. . . The enemy is now mobile.*
> Peter Mayle

Crawling!! Time to rearrange the furniture, remove
fragile objects, and prepare to be on guard duty every
second of the day.

We don't realize how easy we have it until our baby
starts to crawl. Before, we could keep track of him, now
he's halfway across the living room about to pull the lamp
down on his head before we can turn around. We used to
be able to answer the phone, fix dinner, even take a
shower in peace; now everything's fair game, and it's up
to us to have eyes in the back of our head.

Like every milestone it's a blessing and a curse. We
celebrate each step forward and rise to the occasion.

Affirmation: It's a whole new ball game.

Respect

Children may be shorter, but that doesn't mean they're dumber.

Frank Zappa

The infamous rock musician has very definite beliefs about children's innate intelligence, including serious criticisms regarding the "numbing" aspects of traditional education.

While I disagree with his more radical ideas, I wholeheartedly approve of his assertion that children's short stature has no bearing on their mental depths. Children—even tiny babies—should be spoken to respectfully, using language that assumes their comprehension, rather than talking down to them or continually babbling to them in baby talk. (Some cooing and gooing is allowed.)

Since we don't really know how much they understand, we're wise to assume they understand everything. That way, even if they barely come up to our knee, we can't possibly go over their heads.

Affirmation: I respect my child's innate intelligence.

Cereal

> *My life is filled with cereal.*
> *Phyllis McGinley*

Rice cereal. Oatmeal. Froot Loops with stickers at the bottom of the box. Cereal, which seems a constant yet everchanging aspect of childhood, is a great metaphor for parenting.

Cereal is ordinary—as are the daily ups and downs of raising children. Cereal is comforting—as is the nurturing relationship between parents and children. And most cereal is sugary—even the healthiest granola has an element of sweetness, not unlike the sweetness we feel as we sit across the kitchen table from our children.

And in its own way, cereal is a yardstick for our children's growth and independence. We feed them the rice cereal. Cheerios is among their first finger foods. And by the time they're five or six, they can tear into the Wheaties box and add the milk themselves.

But don't get too excited. It generally takes ten more years before they put the box back in the cupboard without being told.

Affirmation: I am watching my child grow every day.

Acknowledgment

*There is no limit to the good a person can do, if he (she) does
not care who gets the credit.*
          Paul S. McElroy

Well, that puts an infinite limit on the good a mother
can do, seeing as we rarely get credit for even a fraction of
our noble deeds.

Acknowledgment is important. It's not *why* we give, it
may not make the giving any easier, but it sure is motivating to know that our acts are noticed and appreciated,
rather than taken for granted. Because if we give and give
and give without any credit at all, after a while we give
reluctantly and resentfully instead of gladly from our
hearts.

There are two important aspects to acknowledgment:
giving credit and taking credit. They are interrelated.
Others will only give us credit if we take credit—if we
believe in the importance of what we do and act proud of
it. And the more credit others give us, the easier it is to
take silent credit for the innumerable unspoken acts of
goodness we're responsible for every single day.

Affirmation: I know how much I do.

Sibling Rivalry

*Just as you can have plenty of love for both your mom and
dad, they can have plenty of love for both you and the baby.*
Mr. Rogers

Easy for Mr. Rogers to say. But at *your* house, in *your*
neighborhood, the bigger kid whose supremacy has been
usurped by a brand-new demanding baby may or may not
be reassured.

Here are some other words to try: "I know this is hard
for you," and "For the next fifteen minutes I'll play with
you even if the baby has to wait," and "I love you even
more than before."

Some words not to say: "You used to scream like that
too," and "I thought you wanted to be a big sister!"

Avoid dismissing or rationalizing away the "big-sister
blues." Instead concentrate on anything that supports, reassures, and allows your bigger kid to feel exactly as she
does, letting her know she can be angry at you and the
baby without losing your love.

Affirmation: I have enough love to go around.

Fathers

I have a feeling Warren Beatty is having a baby so he can meet baby-sitters.

David Letterman

Phooey on that!

Maybe I'm overly sentimental, but I'm sure that Warren Beatty is having a baby for one reason and one reason only—so that he can experience the wonders of fatherhood.

David Letterman's joke, however, is emblematic of the sorts of sexist—yes, sexist—assumptions we make about men, especially those of the been-single-forever playboy variety. We simply can't imagine them choosing the commitment and responsibility implicit in parenthood; we'd rather assume (a) they've been pressured into fatherhood via a paternity suit; or (b) they have an insidious ulterior motive that has nothing to do with wanting to love and care for a child.

I recommend we give Warren Beatty—and others of his ilk—the benefit of the doubt. He deserves it. His wife, Annette Bening deserves it. Their child deserves it.

Affirmation: Let's hear it for fathers!

Overprotectiveness

> *Our child will not be raised in tissue paper! We don't even want her to hear the word* princess.
> *Juliana, princess of the Netherlands*

This is not the sort of dilemma most of us share.

At least not at first glance.

But even if we're raising commoners, we struggle with how much tissue paper to wrap our children in so as to keep them safe from the realm of harsh realities.

Some opt for the "hard knocks" school of parenting: Expose kids to the tough stuff as a way of preparing them for real life. Others choose the "shrink-wrap" school, coddling and tightly controlling their children's lives in an effort to keep them safe from the elements.

Neither strategy is successful in the long run. Too many knocks can knock kids out, and plastic Baggies suffocate. Our best bet is to simply wrap our arms around our children and trust that:

Affirmation: They are strong enough to weather the storms.

Wisdom

Your birthdays sweep by . . . yet I feel less than half as wise as I pretended to be on that birthday when you wailed me into motherhood.

Rita Freedman

Isn't it strange how our wisdom decreases in direct proportion to our children's birthdays?

To commence parenting at all, we need a certain amount of bravado—a pure, confident belief in our capacity to mother, based on nothing more than hubris and hope.

Or maybe with experience comes a greater wisdom— the wisdom that tells us just how much we really don't know, just how much is really involved in being a good parent.

It's probably best that our bravado is greatest in the beginning, when we most need it. Before we really understand the full scope of what we've taken on.

Affirmation: I still have a lot to learn.

Grounding

> *There are times I feel so close to the edge, I could easily tip over.*
>
> *Jessica Lange*

Before you say to yourself, "Boy, I know just how she feels, that's where I'm at after a day with my children," listen to the rest of what Jessica Lange has to say. "If it weren't for the kids, I could very well be gone, emotionally or physically. They've been my salvation."

Well! There's a turnabout! As much as they exhaust, deplete, and overwhelm us, our children are also our grounding. They give us perspective when we're out of focus, they calm us when we're out of control, and they remind us of our holiest purpose when we lose sight of what matters and what our lives are really about.

Affirmation: Being a mother helps keep me sane.

Love

Do you have any idea how much I love you?
All mothers

As much as the ocean? As much as the heavens? As much as all the jelly beans lined up in a row from one end of the earth to the other and then back again?

What mother hasn't said these words—over and over—to her child? And what child could possibly begin to comprehend the depth and breadth of a mother's love?

Yet mothers must say it, perhaps as an attempt, however limited and qualified, to express the immensity of what we feel. And whether or not our children believe or understand what we say, it comforts them to hear our declarations of love.

Affirmation: Do you have any idea how much I love you?

Struggling

> *We give our children the privilege of struggling.*
> Mary Susan Miller

Sometimes it doesn't seem like much of a gift. We grit our teeth watching our children fall down, get hurt, and then get up again. We clench our fists in fear and frustration, wishing fervently we could somehow short-circuit their suffering.

Yet it's the only way they learn. And the best way they grow.

Think of your own struggles. The hardest times often yield the greatest lessons. The same is true of our children. Even though it hurts, sometimes we can only grow stronger the hard way.

Affirmation: Struggling teaches my child inner strength.

Praise

Praise them a lot. They live on it like bread and butter.
Lavina Christensen Fugal

In our parents' day conventional wisdom advised against praising children too much. Compliments were kept to a minimum for fear of raising kids with swelled heads who didn't think there was room for improvement.

Those beliefs, however well meaning, backfired badly. Rather than being conceited, many of us now struggle with low self-esteem. Our parents would have been better advised to praise us lavishly rather than meting out approval in so miserly a fashion. We'd be more confident adults—and more effective parents ourselves—if *our* parents had made as big a deal of our achievements as our failings.

There are plenty of people out there to criticize our children. From us they need praise. And plenty of it.

Affirmation: Have I told my child today how wonderful she is?

Messes

> *A man finds out what is meant by spitting image when he tries to feed cereal to his infant.*
> *Imogene Fey*

Simma, the nineteen-year-old who cared for Zoe when she was an infant, still talks about the Gerber's squash—squishy, orange-colored mush—that dripped down her clothes after a morning feeding the baby.

It's a mess! Yet we take pleasure and pride with each new spoonful of ground, pureed, and half-solid food our child eats and spits out. And as he graduates from breast milk to baby carrots to junior chicken with vegetables, we congratulate him and we congratulate ourselves. For his growth. For our patience. And mostly for the relief that, little by little, there's more ending up in the mouth than on the floor.

Affirmation: It's worth the mess.

Gifts

Glued to the top of the box are twenty-three X's and O's made out of macaroni . . . the treasures of King Tut are nothing in the face of this.
  Robert Fulghum

If you don't yet have any of the precious treasures Robert Fulghum refers to as "gummy lumps," just you wait. Kid cards: the gluey handmade valentines with candy hearts and Mother's Day tributes with scraps of mismatched fabric and the eloquently scrawled message: "I Luv You."

These are the best gifts we ever, ever get. They're the rewards of motherhood. Look forward to them. Save them. Cherish them. They're one-of-a-kind and made with the absolute greatest of care.

Affirmation: I treasure my children's handmade gifts.

Self-forgiveness

If you haven't forgiven yourself something, how can you forgive others?

Dolores Huerta

Most of us live with some skeletons in our closet: stupid mistakes, haunting regrets, amends never made that still weigh heavily on our hearts.

As parents it's especially imperative to forgive ourselves the past. If we can't, we are severely limited in our capacity to accept and forgive our children for the mistakes they make and will continue to make in the future.

If we are compassionate with ourselves, we will focus a less critical—and far more loving eye—on our children. They will come to understand—by way of our example —that being fallible makes them no less lovable.

Affirmation: I forgive myself—and my children— for mistakes made.

A Day in the Life

You've just nursed again. You've read The Velveteen
Rabbit *sixteen times, watched* The Care Bears *video twice,
and played Patty Cake so many times, you're starting to clap
in your sleep. Your husband comes in, trips over the pile of
unfolded laundry in the entryway, and snarls,* "How come
dinner isn't ready?"

Don't say anything.
Count to ten. Then twenty.
Now calmly hand him the baby and suggest he start
cooking.

What about changing into his jeans? Forget it. (When's
the last time you worried about what you were wearing?)
A shower? It can wait. (When's the last time you took a
leisurely shower?) The newspaper? (He'll find it under the
load of laundry when he's finished folding.)

A harsh solution? Maybe. But on the other hand it may
be the only way to get him to see why dinner's late.

If you're in a more conciliatory mood, try educating
him instead. Explain what it's like to be home with the
baby, and be sure to include all the "little" things, such as
changing dozens of diapers, arranging and rearranging
furniture, and making sure the baby doesn't choke, cry
more than five minutes, or have a head-on collision with
any number of dangerous objects all around.

If he still asks "Where's dinner?" go back to Plan A.
After the first half hour on duty, he'll never ask again.

Affirmation: Give me a break!

Paradoxes

> *You begin to understand paradox: lying on the bed next to him, you are deeply interested, and yet at the same time you are deeply bored.*
>
> *Lydia Davis*

This is only one of many paradoxes present in motherhood. We love being with our children, yet we can't wait for the baby-sitter to arrive. We wish time would stop dead in its tracks, yet we anxiously wait for our children to grow up. Being with them makes us feel simultaneously older *and* younger, fearful *and* hopeful, rich *and* poor, often in the very same instant.

There is nothing contradictory about these seemingly opposite feelings. Both sides are true. Thankfully overall our fascination exceeds our boredom. Which is why, paradoxically, we're able to spend hours staring at our child while thinking about all the other things we have to do.

Affirmation: All of my feelings—however seemingly contradictory—make sense.

Infancy

I didn't have a baby in order to have a baby, I had a baby in order to have a child.

Carole Itter

So many people feel this way!

If you're one of them, don't feel guilty and don't despair. There's nothing wrong with preferring older kids; lots of mothers adore the cuddly newborn stage while plenty of others relate better to kids who can carry on a conversation and engage in lots of activities—in other words once they're more of person.

Not adoring babies won't hamper your ability to nurture. And the good (or bad) news is: However you feel, your infant will inevitably grow into a baby, a toddler, and eventually even a teenager. If it's a child you had in mind, just give it time. He or she is on the way.

Affirmation: All babies grow into children.

Affection

Don't be afraid to kiss your baby when you feel like it.
Dr. Benjamin Spock

In fact don't be afraid to kiss your baby even when you *don't* feel like it!

There's no such thing as too much affection, except in the rare case when mothers are overly involved as a way of meeting needs that should only be expressed in adult relationships, in which case counseling is advised.

But most moms lavish kisses and hugs on their children as a spontaneous expression of love. Kisses go a long way with kids. Sometimes they tickle, sometimes they soothe. Often they're better than words. Especially when our children are tiny, holding them closely and planting sweet, warm kisses on their forehead is one of many ways we say:

Affirmation: I adore you!

Arsenic Hour

Between the nap and the twilight
When blood sugar is beginning to lower,
Comes a pause in the day's occupations.
That is known as the Arsenic Hour.
Anonymous

It's the hour dreaded by most mothers. Dusk falls, exhaustion creeps up on us, our baby wakes up from her nap and screams for attention just as we're rushing to put the house in order and get dinner on the table. There are days when arsenic seems like a good idea!

Here are a few better ideas:

1. *Get help.* Hire a neighborhood teenager to play with the baby from four to six, long enough to give you a little breathing room.

2. *Adjust naptime.* There's no rule that says your baby must sleep from two to four. Try keeping her up a little longer and putting her down a little later.

3. *Nap when your baby naps.* Instead of trying to get everything done during naptime, rest when the baby does so you're refreshed and energetic in the late afternoon.

4. *Eat.* Fruit or a high-protein snack—peanut butter or cheese and crackers—will give you a boost to help tide you over. Avoid sweets.

Although there's no magic potion to dilute the Arsenic Hour, doing everything possible to make it easier on yourself helps tide you over till you get a second wind.

Affirmation: There are ways to soften this time of day.

Manners

> *No matter how deep your love, you won't enjoy his company much if he depends on you for everything—and then doesn't bother to say thanks.*
> Marguerite Kelly and Elia Parsons

Miss Manners says—and I wholeheartedly agree—that it's never too early to teach our children to say thank you.

There are two ways to instruct them in this most basic social grace. First, by insisting they say thank you whenever we help them or give them anything. Second, by remembering to always say thank you ourselves.

Start now. When you hand your baby a cracker, remind him to say thank you. (Most toddlers think it's a great game!) He may not understand the meaning of the words quite yet, but sooner or later he'll catch on. And when he hands you his soggy cracker or brings you a book to read, be sure you remember to say, with great enthusiasm, "Thank you!"

Affirmation: Manners matter.

Personal Growth

Children are thrown into the works to make sure you're not getting too stagnant.
                                        Susan Sarandon

Children are great at giving us that proverbial "kick in the pants."

During pregnancy, in anticipation of becoming parents, we redefine our goals and values. Once our children begin to ask questions on their own, we're constantly on our toes—reexamining our beliefs, asking ourselves again and again who we are and what we stand for.

What great insurance against stagnation. We improve our own eating habits so that our children will be healthier, educate ourselves so that we can keep up with them at school, explore our spirituality so that we can guide them in their journey. We, too, grow up and move on. There's just no way to stand still.

Affirmation: Motherhood is a great opportunity for self-improvement.

Equal Parenting

I just don't understand. I mean, women have been having babies for thousands of years and you'd think it would have gotten easier.
     Gary Shepard, thirtysomething

So says novice TV father Gary, after spending hours waiting for his child to be born. Guess what, Gary—women *have* been having and caring for babies for thousands of years, and it isn't any easier than it's ever been.

Newborns are incredibly hard work! It's constant maintenance, nonstop nurturing, and when they finally take a nap, there's loads of laundry and piles of toys to pick up.

The only thing that makes motherhood any easier is fatherhood. Men like Gary on *thirtysomething* who participate fully in parenting, with no illusions about just how much work is really involved.

Affirmation: There's nothing easy about this job.

Weaning

I tried all the conventional ruses (pumping my breasts, drinking beer, eating potatoes) but my milk supply gradually and remorselessly dried up. I felt that I had failed.
Sylvia Ann Hewlett

This confession by scholar and author Sylvia Hewlett makes me sad. How many other new mothers have felt exactly the same sense of failure when, despite their best efforts, nursing simply didn't work out?

If you've given everything you've got to breast-feeding, but for some reason it isn't turning out to be right for you or your baby, then give it up without feeling guilty.

If anything, give yourself credit. Count every single day of nursing as a great gift you've given your baby. Remember the times it was tough, as well as your pleasure and satisfaction. And know that you have been nothing less than a great success.

Affirmation: I did my best.

Making Memories

> *I'm in the business of making memories.*
> Anonymous mother

Last night the 1992 presidential elections were held. At ten-thirty P.M. Central Time the results were announced: Governor Bill Clinton of Arkansas is the next president of the United States of America.

I was thrilled. But what thrilled me even more was watching my children's faces as the returns came in. Watching them decorate the house with red-white-and-blue streamers and stick tiny American flags in cupcakes in preparation for our election party. Watching them witness—and take part in—a moment of history they will never, ever forget.

Last night was a once-in-a-lifetime chance in the memory-making business. I'm *so* glad I didn't miss it.

Affirmation: I am making memories with my children.

A Day in the Life

The mail arrives—an invitation to a Superbowl party given by your closest friend. You call to RSVP, adding, "Of course we'll have to bring the baby." A pause, then she replies, "Well, actually we were only planning on adults." The baby is three months old, and you're not ready for baby-sitters. Besides, you're mad. What do you do?

Here are your choices: First try asking politely whether your baby—since she's so young—can be an exception. After all, this is your best friend, it can't hurt to ask.

If the answer is still no, then you have a few other options. You can try a baby-sitter, since eventually you'll want to go places without the baby. You and your husband can take turns, each attending the party for a short while. Or you can politely decline and watch the game at home.

The only option you *don't* have is to bring the baby anyway, or to make this an issue with your friend. Next year consider having the party at *your* house so that you don't have to go through this again.

Affirmation: I have to be willing to compromise.

Milestones

> *You don't want to leave home in the morning and you can't wait to get home at night. She's a year and a half and she's changing all the time.*
>
> John Goodman

Even when we're at peace with our decision to work outside the home, we still dread missing those "Kodak Moments." It's impossible to be there for all of them, especially during the first year, when our baby literally changes hour to hour.

That's where cameras—and video cameras—come in. If you must be absent for extended periods of time, ask your child-care provider to record all significant passages. There's nothing silly about leaving a loaded camera, a tape recorder, or even an hourly journal in which milestones can be recorded. As the commercial says, it's the next best thing to being there.

Affirmation: There are many more milestones ahead.

Exasperation

*"I'm getting divorced, selling the baby, running away," I
inform Miriam.*

Phyllis Chesler

Of course she doesn't mean it, she's just had it, as most
moms feel from time to time.

The word is *desperate*. Desperate for relief from the
nonstop demands of motherhood. Desperate for a break
from the overwhelming sense of responsibility. Desperate
for someone—anyone—to take over even for a few minutes so that we can rest.

Divorce won't help. (We'd still have the baby, only
more of the time.) Selling isn't an option. (We'd never get
enough.) Running away, on the other hand—to a
friend's for tea, to the mall for an hour of window-shop-
ping—can be exactly what's needed. Just long enough to
look forward to mothering again.

**Affirmation: I don't have to be with my child
twenty-four hours a day.**

Approval

> *Don't say, "I love that picture," say, "I can see how high you stood on your tiptoes to paint that yellow bird in the tree."*
>
> Connie Rubenstein

I was shocked when Connie, the child-development expert who lectured our parent-toddler group, made this distinction. Here I thought I was saying the perfect thing; each time my two-year-old drew a picture or picked up her toys, I'd exclaim, "I'm so pleased by what you've done!"

Apparently I was missing the point. When we say, "I like what you did," we give our children the message that our approval is based on their success. When we say, "I can see how hard you tried," or "I bet you feel great about what you've done," we applaud them for their own sense of mastery and satisfaction.

Affirmation: It's the effort that counts.

Balance

A problem of balance: If he yawns, he falls over backward.
Lydia Davis

It's surprising how often the "problem of balance" keeps mothers off center. We struggle to maintain our center of gravity nine-months pregnant, attempting to tie our shoes without tumbling over. We continually lose our balance bending over backward making sure our six-month-old doesn't land on her head. We stand with out-stretched arms as our one-year-old takes his wobbly first step. We watch with trepidation as our five-year-old, carrying the too-big school bag, climbs onto the kindergarten bus.

At each step we shudder at the thought of what will happen if we—or they—lose our balance. At each step we try to stay centered and calm.

Affirmation: I have both feet on the ground.

Respect

> *Childhood is frequently a solemn business for those inside it.*
> George F. Will

It's often tempting to burst out laughing at things our children do: when our one-year-old tries her first somersault and lands on her ear; when our two-year-old asks for "pasghetti" for dinner; when our three-year-old solemnly declares he's running away from home.

Funny as these moments are, it's important to take our children seriously rather than risk hurting their feelings. We can laugh alone, once they're in bed. But while they're in hearing range, we'd best keep our amusement in check.

Affirmation: Even when it's funny, I'll be careful to not laugh at my child.

Monsters

The monster under the bed finally arrived at our house the other night. I've been waiting for him to show up for four years.

Anna Quindlen

It's the rare child who doesn't encounter the "monster," whether it's lurking under the sheets, peeking out of the closet, or slipping in and out of the shadows on the bedroom wall.

Saying "Don't worry, there *is* no monster" may be one of the most common parenting mistakes. For one thing it's a way of talking children out of their very real feelings and perceptions. For another thing it doesn't assuage their fears, it simply drives them underground.

Active strategies for "battling" the monsters are far more successful. A night-light, a magic wand to wave, or a special chant to ward them off can all help children deal with their fears in a positive, empowering way.

Affirmation: Tell me about your monster.

Honesty

> *The second time I lied to my baby, I told him he was the best baby in the world.*
>
> Lydia Davis

This confession is so innocent and so common, it barely even belongs in the "white lie" category.

I've done it too. I tell my kids all the time that they're the best, the smartest, the most wonderful children on the planet.

And why shouldn't we? Rest assured that no matter how far our children go, regardless of how loved they are and how much success they achieve, no one will ever be quite so enchanted with them as we are.

It doesn't matter that most mothers say the very same thing. Think what a better world it would be if every single child grew up feeling just this way.

Affirmation: You're the best baby in the whole world.

Self-preservation

In the case of a crash mothers of young children are advised to fasten their oxygen mask before fastening their child's . . . the same is necessary on terra firma.
Joyce Maynard

No matter how often I fly, I am always surprised by these instructions; in the case of a sudden loss in cabin pressure I just can't imagine fastening my own oxygen mask while my child coughs and gasps and struggles for air.

But as these words from an essay by Joyce Maynard remind us, we can only help our child breathe if we're able to breathe ourselves.

By the same token we can only meet our children's needs when we're attending to our own. This may sound selfish. It may clash with our definition of a good mother as someone who always puts her children first.

On the contrary we need to remember that in normal, as well as tough times, we have to be healthy and whole in order to help our children.

Affirmation: There's a direct correlation between my ability to meet my own needs and my ability to care for my child.

Skills

I know how to do anything. I'm a mom.
　　　　　Roseanne Arnold

I asked several new moms to assess what they've learned so far. Here's a sample list of what they said:
1. Patience
2. Flexibility
3. How to do eight things at once
4. Humor
5. How to build sandcastles
6. All the words to *Pat the Bunny*
7. A dozen different things to do with flour, water, and food coloring

As our child adds to her repertoire of skills, so our own skills grow by leaps and bounds. However, I suspect that Roseanne Arnold isn't only referring to all the things we know how to *do;* she's also referring to the increased self-confidence we gain through motherhood. As we rise to the challenges—finding the stamina to care for a collicky baby or the creativity to keep our two-year-old entertained on the fifth rainy day in a row—we discover how much we know and how much we have to give.

Affirmation: These are three new skills I've learned since having my baby:
1. _____.
2. _____.
3. _____.

Hard Days

After all, tomorrow is another day.
Scarlett O'Hara

We all have "those days." When the baby never naps. When the toddler, like Sherman's Civil War army, demolishes everything in his path. When the three-year-old answers every single question with her favorite new word, *no,* until we wish we could take to our bed and start all over again tomorrow.

We can't go to bed, but tomorrow *will* come. And it will be a better day. Just when we think we can't take another ten minutes of our beloved baby, she surprises us by settling down for a three-hour nap. The toddler involves himself in an extensive Lego construction project. The three-year-old enchants us again with her sweetness and light.

There are "those days." Thankfully.

Affirmation: There's always tomorrow.

Overscheduling

Every day make a commitment to do only one activity.
Experienced mom

These words of advice come from a woman who recently had her third child. "With my first two kids I tried to pack a million things into each day," she recalls. "I'd care for them while cleaning the refrigerator, running errands, and catching up with a friend on the phone. And every day I ended up frustrated and exhausted. So now I only do *one* thing, and anything else that gets accomplished is a bonus."

This is advice well taken. There's no point in running ourselves ragged. Make a list of everything that needs to be done, number it in order of importance, and then only do what's first on the list. If anything else gets finished, great. If not, you're doing enough as it is.

Affirmation: I won't stretch myself too thin.

Criticism

We want daughters-in-law who are going to stay home and raise our grandchildren.

Erma Bombeck

If you're a mom working outside the home, you may experience criticism, subtle or blatant, from your mother or mother-in-law. Sometimes it comes in the form of comparison: "Ruth's daughter, Susie, stays home with *her* baby." Other times it's offered as worrying: "Have you seen the latest studies on how children in day care are much more aggressive?"

Assume that these comments are coming from genuine concern for your child. Which, of course, doesn't diminish your natural feelings of defensiveness. Even if you're perfectly confident that you're doing right by your child, it's easy to feel undermined by a grandmother's judgments.

If such comments really begin to grate on you, it might be time to take a stand. Consider saying "I appreciate your concern, but it would mean a great deal to me if you could support my decision to combine motherhood and a career." In any case take solace in your own belief that you are doing the very best you can for your child and for yourself.

Affirmation: I don't need to defend myself.

Ordinariness

> *Perfection consists not in doing extraordinary things well, but in doing ordinary things extraordinarily well.*
> *Angelique Arnauld*

Every mother should have this quote highly visible somewhere in her home.

Sometimes it's hard to see the importance of all the ordinary tasks performed in the course of a typical day. Hours spent diapering, feeding, playing "How big is the baby?" over and over with our child. Whatever happened to the days spent reading fiction, training for the marathon, knocking ourselves out to get ahead at work, then being able to collapse in a chair once we got home?

There will be plenty of time to do all those things. But for right now the seemingly "ordinary" tasks of motherhood make an extraordinary difference in our child's life.

Affirmation: There is great value in all I give.

Awareness

My parents put a live teddy bear in my crib.
Woody Allen

All joking aside, we live in a culture increasingly focused on blaming parents for problems we struggle with throughout life. It's important to be conscious of ways in which we inadvertently damage our child's self-esteem. But by the same token we can be overly vigilant, censoring our every word and glance for fear that our child will end up hating us, spending a fortune on twenty years of psychotherapy.

The truth is there's no way to avoid making some mistakes, no matter how psychologically savvy we are. What we *can* do, however, is be as honest as possible when we do make a mistake. And make an ongoing commitment to maintaining our own emotional health.

Affirmation: I'll try to be as conscious as I can.

Fatherhood

Spock, schlock . . . a man doesn't know how to bring up children until he's been a mother.
Dan Greenberg

Clearly there's nothing like a mother. But then there's nothing like a father either. Both mothers *and* fathers are essential—and equally important—in raising children! Given our cultural conditioning, men and women may parent differently, both in how and in what we give. But for anyone to imply that women are inherently more capable or necessary is a big step backward for fathers, who in the past decades have made such important strides in assuming greater involvement in their children's lives.

Let's hope that in the foreseeable future mothers and fathers will be equally capable and equally appreciated. Now there would be a great leap forward for us all.

Affirmation: Fathers are just as important as mothers.

Noise

Having children is like having a bowling alley installed in your brain.

> Martin Mull

Have you ever noticed how parents of grown children talk about how quiet it is once their kids leave home?

Small children are incredibly noisy. We become inured to the clatter, yet it still takes its toll. The high decibel level makes us crabby and frustrated, which is why it's so important to remove ourselves occasionally from the chaos to hear ourselves think.

Find a relatively quiet place—even if it's the bathroom —where you can escape from the din. Just a few moments of silence is soothing and helps make you able to return to the fray.

Affirmation: Someday I'll look back and miss the clatter.

Distraction

> *That day I was desperate. I dragged them out to my car in the*
> *pouring rain, put them in the back seat, and told them, "Stay*
> *there and play car wash."*
> Lily Tomlin and Jane Wagner

It reminds me of the time I set Evan, then six, up with
twenty-five lottery tickets to scratch off and organize in
piles in order to score an extra half hour of sleep.

Although our children would love for us to be with
them every single second, there's simply no way to fulfill
such a fantasy. When we need a break, we need a break,
and there's nothing wrong with that, especially if we can
find some creative distraction to occupy their attention.

A little time apart is good for mothers and children.
After all, absence makes the heart grow fonder, and we
come back refreshed and ready to spend quality time.

Affirmation: We all have our days.

Firstborns

The first child is kind of like the first pancake. If it's not perfect, there are a lot more coming along.
Antonin Scalia

First—or only—children are a bit like subjects in an experiment. With them we learn to be parents, test our theories, and make our mistakes, and, more often than not, make our most intense demands.

This can be a real double-edged sword. While first kids get the benefit of our concentrated devotion, they also bear the burden of our most rigid expectations. We watch their every move with baited breath, exclaiming over their bowel movements, their first, glorious words, their every achievement. So often first children go on to be unusually high achievers, motivated by underlying feelings of pressure to gain parental approval.

We must be careful to love our first children without pressuring them. Like the first pancake, they needn't be perfect in order to be just right.

Affirmation: I'll try to relax my expectations.

Approval

> *The secret ingredient of fatherhood is approval.*
> Ellen Goodman

Likewise, the secret—and perhaps most important—ingredient of motherhood is approval.

Giving children our strong approval is a way of saying, "I love you even when I don't agree with you."

This is easier said than done. Even with the best of intentions, most parents fall into the trap of wanting a child to do what *we* want, to be who *we* think he or she should be, to make the choices *we* feel are best.

Yet, from the time they're small, whether it's choosing a puzzle instead of the book we've waited to read them, making a friend we don't particularly care for, or insisting on a checks-and-stripes combination that makes us cringe, we continually face the challenge of giving our approval and giving up our impulse to control.

Our children want us to approve. They need us to. If we can give them this one thing—and on terms that are meaningful to them—we provide the foundation for them to go out into the world with a deep sense of confidence and security.

Affirmation: I approve.

A Day in the Life

You've just finished sharing a lovely Sunday dinner with your parents when your two-year-old daughter points to her diaper and says, "My vagina!" Your mother turns white. Your father leaves the room looking as if he's about to throw up. You don't want to start anything, but you do want to acknowledge your daughter's correct use of words. What do you do?

First turn to your daughter, smile, and say, "That's right, honey. That's your vagina."

Now for your parents. You may or may not want to get into what is clearly a generational gap. This depends on how close you are, how important it is to make them see your point of view, and most important whether or not you're concerned that they may give your child the message that it's wrong to be proud of all the parts of her body and call them by their appropriate names.

This may be a conflict you choose to ignore. However, if you feel strongly about speaking up, simply say, "It's common these days to try to use the correct names."

Enough said.

Affirmation: Every generation parents a little differently.

Tolerance

Don't gossip about the children of others while yours are still growing up.

Jewish proverb

It's tempting to compare and gossip, especially about children of neighbors or close friends. It's a matter of comfort—and relief—to know that someone else's child isn't walking yet or struck a playmate or is having trouble with arithmetic; these little bits of news make us feel a little better about our own child being less than perfect.

But gossip is damaging—and dangerous. We risk spreading nasty rumors and hurting others. Being superstitious, I prefer to censor my criticisms, knowing full well that someday *my* child may be the one being whispered about behind closed doors. Since our own children will inevitably screw up, it's safer—and kinder—to say only nice things and keep our judgments to ourselves.

Affirmation: I'll resist the urge to gossip about other people's children.

Encouragement

Treat people as if they were what they ought to be and you help them become what they are capable of being.
Goethe

Sage advice for parents.

Giving our children encouragement—"You're doing great!" or "Why don't you give it a try?"—are ways of gently motivating them to stretch their limits and fulfill their capabilities.

Too often we give them a message of discouragement out of our desire to protect them. We're afraid they'll be disappointed if they try and fail.

But the real failure is not having the courage to try. We give our children a critical gift—the gift of confidence—when we respect their inner strength, their resiliency, and their ability to rise to challenges, whether they win or lose.

Affirmation: You can do it!

Smiles

> *There's this moment when your baby cries and you pick her up and suddenly she's all smiles—it's magic.*
> *Hope Steadman (thirtysomething)*

There is something so incredibly magical about our baby's smiles. When his face crinkles up and breaks into that inimitable grin, all the work and energy is suddenly worthwhile.

Smiles are our reward for all the hard work. For the crying we can't seem to do anything about. For the times when we're out of patience and seemingly out of luck. Then they smile.

Even though we're no more responsible for our children's joy than we are for their sorrow, when they smile, *we* smile. In fact everything in the room seems to smile, illuminated by the beauty and light radiating from our child.

Affirmation: What a great reward!

Acceptance

The thing you learn about children is that you can't change them.

Mick Jagger

Our baby loves his pacifier and we keep trying to introduce him to his thumb. Our toddler stands apart during "circle time" at nursery school and we jump through hoops trying to get her to join in. Our three-year-old couldn't care less about the swimming lessons we keep dragging him to; our four-year-old picks out frilly dresses instead of the jeans and sweatshirts we want to bring home.

Our children are who they are, not necessarily who we want them to be. This is the great challenge of parenting: to love our children enough to leave them alone.

Affirmation: Acceptance is a form of love.

Discoveries

> *No one shows a child the sky.*
> *African proverb*

I find this a most reassuring proverb.

It reminds me that no matter how awesome the responsibilities of parenthood, there are some very important things children learn all on their own.

Like the fact that the first snowfall tastes great, especially with sugar and red food coloring. And the fact that tree branches bend but are hard to break. And hands held over flashlights make incredible shapes on the ceiling. And the sky at night isn't really black, but some indefinable blend of purple and blue.

We can teach them to read. To eat cereal with a spoon. To lace their shoes and button their jackets. But so many important things simply have their own ways of showing themselves to a child.

Affirmation: I'm not my child's only teacher.

Presents

Everything positive you have ever taught your child will evaporate when it's time to open the presents.
Anna Quindlen

Our perfectly civilized darlings turn into barbarians the moment we place a pile of birthday or holiday gifts in front of them.

But don't try to fight it. Until a child is five or six, it's unrealistic to expect them to calmly open each gift and sweetly say thank you. Tearing wrapping paper, wildly tossing ribbons and bows, exclaiming, "I've already *got* this!" and rushing to the next gift without acknowledging the last is much more likely to occur. This has nothing to do with manners or values. It doesn't mean you're doing a rotten job of raising your child.

Even the most well-mannered children behave this way. (As did most of their parents.) We can avoid tearing hair out over this if we simply remember:

Affirmation: My child's "present" behavior will pass.

Baby-proofing

> *You can disarm the coffee table by clearing off the top and taping foam rubber padding 'round the sharp edges . . . this style is known as "Infant Provincial."*
> Peter Mayle

If your baby is mobile—or even edging toward the furniture—it's time to baby-proof.

Some parents' idea of baby-proofing is shrieking "no!!!" every time their child comes within reaching distance of precious objects. Not the best approach. This is one situation in which it's wiser to adapt the environment to the child.

For one thing, you get hoarse constantly screaming no. For another thing it can't help but make your child feel bad about doing exactly what he *should* be doing at this stage—exploring with a relatively free rein. And, replacement costs being what they are, your valuables are much safer on a high shelf than within your baby's grasp.

Affirmation: Baby proofing is good protection all around.

Bedtime

The best time for parents to put the children to bed is while they still have the strength.
Homer Phillips

I remember once being amazed when some friends of ours, parents of small children, remarked (rather smugly, I believe) that their kids were put to bed promptly at six-thirty each night.

As someone who struggles to get dinner served and cleaned up before eight, I was intrigued and envious at the idea of a peaceful, child-free evening in which to dine, read, and spend time with my husband. But I was also a little concerned at the loss of what I consider one of the nicest parts of the day: family time around the dinner table, watching television, downtime when we all relax and catch up and enjoy ourselves.

Whether you put your child to bed on a strict schedule, keep her up till she drops, or something in between, the point is to keep bedtime from becoming a battle between exhausted children and equally exhausted grown-ups. One thing I've learned: Start bedtime at least forty-five minutes before your goal. Build in the fudge factor of extra trips to the bathroom, last-minute sips of water, and terribly important conversations that can only take place just when it's time to tuck 'em in.

Affirmation: Good night.

Fantasies

> *Ariel: I imagine all the ways I can kill you.*
> *I can drown you in the bathtub.*
> *I can smother you with a pillow.*
> *I can bang your head on the floor; once, hard.*
> Phyllis Chesler

Before you call Child Protection in horror at this mother's apparent infanticidal tendencies, think about the times you've caught yourself fantasizing the same.

The operative word here is *fantasy*. And there's a good reason why most mothers are visited by such horrible thoughts. It's a way of coming to terms with how incredibly fragile our children are and how unimaginably heartbroken we would be if something happened to them.

Don't be frightened by fantasies of this sort. Just as you let yourself feel your immense joy, allow yourself to imagine the unspeakable. It's simply a reminder of how easily our precious babies could be broken. A sign of how deeply we love them and how awesome is the responsibility for their care.

Affirmation: At times my love for my child is overwhelming.

Adjustments

Infancy conforms to nobody; all conform to it.
   Ralph Waldo Emerson

By this time you've probably noticed that your life is no longer your own. You jump when your child cries, you organize your schedule around his needs, you sleep whenever you can, you make forays out into the world only after making elaborate arrangements for holding down the fort.

This is how it is to be a parent of small children. We conform to their style and pace, and sometimes we resent it. We yearn for the past, when we had the luxury of coming and going as we pleased, eating when we felt like it, following our own desires and goals without always accommodating another person—an uncompromising one at that.

The good news is the older our kids get, the less we must conform. With age they're more patient, more flexible, and less tyrannical in their needs.

It's worth the wait. And by the time it comes, we really appreciate it.

Affirmation: This won't last forever.

Friendship

Our life was one long conversation about how tiring our days were.

Roberta Israeloff

Written shortly after her son, Ben, was born, these words describe Roberta Israeloff's relationship with her husband in the early days of motherhood.

Romantic? No. Intimate? Hardly. Her description is typical of the frustration so many new parents feel trying to connect in the wake of birth, sleepless nights, and demanding days with an infant.

Is it inevitable for our most important adult relationship to be reduced to this?

Yes and no. On the one hand it's realistic during these first weeks and months to adjust expectations and be gentle with each other. Both parents are making a huge adjustment; it's natural to yearn for our past romantic relationship.

On the other hand there are ways, even in the midst of all this, to enhance intimacy. Listening without criticism. Supporting each other to take time off. Recognizing and thanking each other for the contributions we are each making to our newly enlarged family. Sharing hopes and fears, along with the details of our day—however tiring—helps us to stay connected and close.

Affirmation: Let's help each other through this time.

A Day in the Life

It's been a perfect day. The baby went down for two three-hour naps, you got all the laundry done, returned business calls, and still had time to finish reading a novel. Now what's so hard about being a mother?

Nothing, on days like this, when everything goes just right.

Every day has its own rhythm, its own challenges. Some days are impossible; everything that can go wrong does go wrong. Then there are idyllic days when being a mother is everything wonderful we ever imagined and more.

The trick is to expect both ups and downs, hard days and easy days, times when motherhood makes us wring our hands in frustration along with days when we can't believe how lucky we are. As long as the hard days don't throw us, the easy days are perfect opportunities to stop for a moment, close our eyes, and say:

Affirmation: Thank you for this perfect day.

Spontaneity

> *The essence of pleasure is spontaneity.*
> Germaine Greer

Forget planning. Relinquish your fantasy of the three-hour nap your baby will take at exactly two P.M. Throw away the list of everything you need to do today—grocery shopping, checking in at the office, writing thank-you notes for baby gifts—because it probably won't happen.

When we try to plan and control our day with a new baby, we're bound to get upset. We spend precious energy being angry over a timetable that's out of our hands instead of saving our energy to handle what's right in front of us.

If we can relax our expectations, we minimize frustration and increase our capacity to enjoy the moments of unexpected pleasure—and peace—that befall us.

Affirmation: I'm learning to roll with the punches.

Responsibility

Tonight I see how scared I am. There is so much to do for this little creature who screams and wriggles.
David Steinberg

It's great to hear a new dad express the feelings of fear that most all moms experience at some time.

It *is* scary, especially when we acknowledge how utterly fragile and dependent our baby is. Especially when we realize the full impact of being absolutely responsible for his or her survival.

It gets less scary. Or maybe we just get more confident and sure of our ability to care for our child. And as each day passes, we become more sure that our child is safe and sound and here to stay.

Affirmation: My fears are perfectly natural to feel.

Being in Charge

> *The decision to eat strained lamb or not eat strained lamb should be with the feedee not the feeder.*
> Erma Bombeck

Spoken with the wisdom of one who's cleaned up more than her share (three children's worth to be exact) of strained lamb.

But what Erma Bombeck, in her inimitably humorous way, is really talking about is *who* gets to be in charge—mother or child?

Too often we allow our children to call the shots. They spit out strained lamb, we make them creamed carrots. They refuse to play with the Legos, we run out and buy them the Fisher-Price Zoo they've been begging for. They say "another half hour, pleeeeeeze" in that plaintive tone, and we give in again, even though it's way past bedtime.

Kids need a certain amount of discipline and structure. So saying no, saying "my way," saying it's strained lamb or nothing, is neither cruel nor autocratic. It's a parent's imperative, one that should be taken seriously and used wisely.

Affirmation: It's a mother's prerogative.

Pediatricians

"There's nothing to worry about" is a typical example of the kind of easy-for-you-to-say remarks that pediatricians like to make.

Dave Barry

Contrary to popular belief, they don't say that because they're insensitive, too busy, or cavalier about your child's health and well-being. In most cases pediatricians say "there's nothing to worry about" because, based on years of experience, they truly believe there's no cause for concern.

Which does nothing to alleviate a mother's fears. In fact it may make things worse. When our child is fluish or feverish or merely under the weather, the last thing we want is to be dismissed with such seemingly casual reassurance. We want our child's symptoms taken seriously; we want every inch examined, every symptom explored in full.

Being told there's nothing to worry about—once, twice, a hundred times—is no reason to stop asking. *We* know our child best. If there was nothing to worry about, we wouldn't be at the doctor's.

Affirmation: I will trust my pediatrician, but not at the expense of my own judgment.

Baby Talk

> *My wife and I often summoned the grandparents of our first baby and cried, "Look. Poopoo!"*
> Bill Cosby

What is it about babies that makes otherwise intelligent adults babble nonsensically?

They're just *so* cute! Everything about them is cute, even their bowel movements, which we talk about enthusiastically at the drop of a hat.

The truth is, no one but parents care. Even the most doting grandparents at best indulge us in our endless up-to-the-minute reports, which often include several poopoo references.

The need to convey such detailed personal information is a passing stage, best shared with other new parents, who understand.

Affirmation: I'll keep the details to a minimum.

Loving

The giving of love is an education in itself.
Eleanor Roosevelt

From this standpoint all mothers should receive doctorates!

We know that we are in the business of educating our children, yet rarely do we recognize how much we, too, are learning in the process.

What do we learn from giving love? We learn to be generous of spirit—to tap a deep inner source of strength even when we feel tired and depleted.

We learn to be unconditionally accepting—to support our child even when we don't understand or agree.

We learn to be unselfish—to put someone else's needs ahead of our own.

And beyond all else, we learn how loving we really are.

Affirmation: Motherhood is a constant lesson in love.

Exhaustion

> *No animal is so inexhaustible as an excited infant.*
> *Amy Leslie*

We get to the end of the day and can't figure out why we're so completely exhausted. After all, all we did was spend the day taking care of our child. What's so hard about that?

Wait a minute. Review the last twelve hours. A typical day with a newborn: up at dawn after a few hours sleep, six diaper changes, five feedings, and three aborted nap attempts interspersed with numerous mystifying crying spells. A typical day with a toddler: a high-speed chase behind a whirlwind of motion about to crash into everything in its path. A typical day with a two-year-old: finding the puzzle, assembling the puzzle, searching for puzzle pieces, consoling hysterical puzzle-putter-together after puzzle piece doesn't fit, try another puzzle. . . .

It's enough to make anyone exhausted!

Affirmation: I've earned my exhaustion.

Evolution

One is not born a woman, one becomes one.
    Simone de Beauvoir

The same is true of motherhood. We're not born with the feelings or the skills that are necessary to be a good mother. No, we gradually learn how to mother.

It takes time, years of time. As we come to know our child—what each cry means, their likes and dislikes, their special needs and idiosyncrasies—we get better and better at giving them what they need. And as our skills grow, so does our love. With each year they become dearer and dearer to us, and we become more confident in our capacity to nurture and guide.

It doesn't happen overnight. With experience over time we become a mother.

Affirmation: I'm growing into the role.

Gratitude

You have not lived a perfect day unless you have done something for someone who will never be able to repay you.
Ruth Smeltzer

I guess this means that any given day in a mother's life is pretty darn near perfect!!

So much of our relationship with our children is based on giving just because we love them, just because they're children and it's up to us to make sure they're fed and clothed and nourished in every possible way.

There is no repayment. Our children can never give back what we've given them, just as we can never repay the love and generosity of our own parents. Children are not indebted to parents; it is not up to them to justify our love in any way.

Being a parent means giving out of pure love. Our reward is seeing our children become human beings capable of repeating the pattern, giving to others out of the goodness of their hearts.

Affirmation: My child doesn't owe me a thing.

Nurturing

Babies don't need fathers, but mothers do. Someone who is taking care of a baby needs to be taken care of.
    Amy Heckerling

The first part of this quote is questionable; I'd argue that, with the obvious exception of nursing, babies need fathers just as much as they need mothers.

However, the second half of this quote is right on the money. Especially in the first several months of our child's life, mothers need to be mothered. We need loving, and lots of it, not necessarily by a husband but by someone—friends, parents, or lovers—who can replenish the enormous store of energy continually pouring out of us. We need cuddling and massages and good food and tons of support and encouragement.

At this stage of motherhood, baby is not the only one who needs to be "babied" a bit.

Affirmation: I'll let myself be nurtured.

Mentoring

> *We have not sat at the feet of older women and learned from them.*
>
> Barbara Jenkins

Long gone are the days of extended families where new mothers sat at the feet of older women and learned the "motherwit" and folklore and secrets of motherhood gathered over generations.

Today we are mostly on our own. We may collect bits and pieces of information from books or other moms, but we've lost our connection with a valuable store of knowledge only gained from the accumulated voices of experience.

If your mother or grandmother is alive, talk to her.

Or seek out another older woman in your community. Find out what it was like for her to be a mother—her trials and triumphs, the mistakes she made, the lullabyes she sang, her mother's herbal antidote for sniffly noses. Even if some child-raising attitudes are outdated, the wisdom of our elders can teach us so much.

Affirmation: I learn what I can from mothers who have been here before.

Housecleaning

I'm going to clean this dump—just as soon as the kids are grown.

Erma Bombeck

Face it. Children can turn even the most beautifully kept home into a dump within minutes. Their stuff simply oozes out and takes over. Scattered toys, bottles and pacifiers, books and half-chewed graham crackers seem to proliferate before our eyes.

We have two choices: We can try to beat it—and beat ourselves over the head trying to keep a pristine home. Or, we can readjust our expectations and learn to pick our way through the mess.

I recommend a compromise. Figure out what you can live with (toys in one corner and the rest of the room straightened up, the whole place cleaned once a week and in between try not to notice) and let go of your prebaby notion of home beautiful.

It's just not worth agonizing over. You'll have plenty of time to clean—just as soon as the kids are grown.

Affirmation: My home doesn't have to be perfectly immaculate.

Attention

> *Perhaps a child who is fussed over gets a feeling of destiny
> . . . he thinks he is in the world for something important.*
> Dr. Benjamin Spock

Fussing doesn't mean spoiling; it's a way of making our child feel special, cherished, worthy of great and wonderful things.

And fussing doesn't necessarily mean making a big deal of our child. We fuss when we spend fifteen minutes lovingly brushing our daughter's hair. When we pay rapt attention to a painting, a poem, or a bottlecap collection; when we watch the twelfth clumsy cartwheel, exclaiming over our child's effort and charm.

Every child should be fussed over as if he or she is the most terrific child in the world. Perhaps then we'd have a world filled with children who value themselves and who know that they are loved.

Affirmation: My child deserves to be fussed over.

Equal Opportunity

William wants a doll!!!
> Free to Be You and Me

When I was growing up, boys, unless they were "sissies," didn't play with dolls. They played with trucks and Lincoln Logs and squirt guns and toads, while girls spent endless hours dressing their Barbie dolls.

But as this wonderful song from *Free to Be You and Me* expresses, the times have changed. And thank goodness! Today's parents are no longer chained to the gender-based gift-giving traditions of the past. We understand how important it is to encourage our children—boys and girls—to make choices based on their desires, not on stereotypes that limit their creativity.

Let your son have a doll. Let your daughter crash trucks to her heart's content. Neither will be harmed; both will be happier and healthier.

Affirmation: I want my child to have every opportunity regardless of gender.

Grounding

> *Children are the anchors that hold a mother to life.*
> Sophocles

The other day a new mom came to see me for counseling. She spoke of feeling overwhelmed, burnt out, as if she was about to lose it. Sometimes, she wearily confessed, she even contemplated running away and never coming back.

"Of course I never would," she quickly told me, "because of my daughter. But if it weren't for her . . ."

There are times when we feel this way. There are too many demands, not enough time and energy, and we just feel like giving up. But we don't. Why? Because of our children.

We have to keep our head on straight and keep our feet on the ground. We have to handle our responsibilities because our children depend on us. And so, once again, we find the strength within.

Affirmation: Motherhood helps keep me sane.

Self-acceptance

It is impossible for any woman to love her children twenty-four hours a day.
        Milton R. Sapirstein

Okay. Let's admit it. Sometimes we *don't* love them. Or like them. Or even think they're cute. To be perfectly honest, sometimes we wish they belonged to someone else.

Welcome to reality. If you're worried about feeling this way, stop. Every mother, even the most devoted, has her moments, sometimes even hours and days, when this, like anything else, becomes a drudge rather than a labor of love. It doesn't mean we fail to show up for work; it doesn't mean our productivity lessens, it just means that we accept our feelings, put ourselves on automatic pilot, and keep doing a good job.

Affirmation: Love returns. It needn't be present every moment of every day.

Hands

> *The sweetest flowers in all the world—*
> *A baby's hands.*
> Algernon Charles Swinburne

Oh, those hands. Those fragile petals that wrap around our finger, sweeter than the sweetest rose.

Babies' hands are, perhaps, among the purest things on earth. Miracles of nature. So dear, so innocent, they give us goose bumps.

Take a moment, right now if possible, away from your responsibilities, away from your everyday demands, and simply take your baby's hand in your own. Feel its velvety touch. Smell its fragrance. Stroke each tiny finger and hold it close to your cheek. Turn it over a few times and simply notice its sweet perfection, how perfect it is.

Affirmation: Let's hold hands.

A Day in the Life

You've spent the past hour kneeling on the bathroom floor cajoling, bribing, begging your three-year-old to go potty. You give up. Five minutes later his training pants are soaked. You're frustrated. Worried. If he's not trained, they won't let him into preschool. What are you going to do?

Nothing. You're going to do exactly nothing.

It's frustrating when our children don't perform "on schedule," especially when somebody else's timetable is breathing down our neck.

But experts agree that there is a wide range of acceptable potty-training time; the less we force it, the greater our chances of success.

A calm, casual attitude is what's needed here. Positive reinforcement is fine, as long as you are careful to not shame or pressure your child. When he's ready, he'll give up diapers.

Affirmation: I'll try not to push.

Role Models

> *This would be a better world for children if parents had to eat the spinach.*
>
> > Groucho Marx

Or at least if parents ate the spinach alongside their kids.

We can't expect our children to develop healthful eating habits—or any other good habits, for that matter—if we're not willing to do the same. They learn to wear seatbelts by seeing us consistently fasten our own; they learn to clean up after themselves by watching us keep our own belongings in order.

It's only fair. And it's the best way to guarantee our children's turning out the way we hope.

Affirmation: I'll try to be a positive role model.

Limitations

> *This is the Basic Baby Mood Cycle:*
> *Mood One: Just about to cry.*
> *Mood Two: Crying.*
> *Mood Three: Just finished crying.*
>   *Dave Barry*

There's nothing especially amusing about those days when it seems all our baby does is cry, cry some more, and cry until he collapses from exhaustion, only to wake up crying again, all for no apparent reason.

Maybe it's colic. Maybe it's teething. Maybe we'll never know. But even when we feel sure that our baby is all right, it's hard to listen to the constant wail without feeling helpless, frustrated, and ready to burst into tears ourselves.

The crying *will* stop. Gradually babies cry less and less, and when they do cry, what's needed is usually apparent. In the meantime intervals of silence are music to our ears.

Affirmation: Sometimes there just isn't anything I can do.

Patience

> *Have patience with all things, but first of all with yourself.*
> *Saint Francis of Sales*

It's easy to feel frustrated with ourselves when we're crabby with our children, when we fail to anticipate their needs, when we fall short of our expectations of what it means to be a good mother.

We can spend the next twenty years counting our mistakes. Or we can accept our limitations and learn to be patient with ourselves.

It isn't easy to be a parent; in fact it's one of the most complex challenges in the world. Perfection isn't required; we needn't get it right all or even most of the time. All that's asked is our best effort and the willingness to give ourselves plenty of rope.

Affirmation: I'll be patient with myself.

Child Raising

Children should be seen and not heard.
Anonymous

So many of the child-raising beliefs we were raised with are now up for grabs: Children should be seen and not heard. A "good child" always does what his parents say. Father knows best . . . even when he doesn't.

Today we know that children should be encouraged to express themselves, that compliance isn't always appropriate, that parents don't always know best, that in fact our children can often point out a better way.

As parents it's important to ask ourselves whether long-standing "words of wisdom" are truly wise, whether they actually contribute to our children's healthy development and positive self-esteem.

It's up to each of us to decide for ourselves. Just because *our* parents did it doesn't make it right.

Affirmation: Children should be seen and heard.

Self-trust

> *Trust your hunches.*
> ### Dr. Joyce Brothers

Jacob, Bonnie's six-week-old baby, just didn't seem right to her. Even though he wasn't running a temperature, she took him to the doctor, and sure enough he had viral pneumonia.

There's just something about a mother's hunches; we know our child, we notice the subtle ways in which he or she is upset or worried or under the weather.

Trusting our hunches doesn't mean we ignore expert advice or always think we're right. It just means that when it comes to our child, we take our own perceptions seriously and listen to our heart.

Affirmation: I know my child best.

Social Activism

You can't hug your child with nuclear arms.
Bumper sticker

No matter how often I see it, this bumper sticker always makes me stop and think: about the possibility of destroying the future; about the violence and danger in our midst; about the imperative for parents to take a strong stand and actively work to create a safer, more peaceful world.

Each of us can make a difference. And each of us must do what we can. Our children's survival depends on it.

Affirmation: I'm committed to creating a safe, peaceful world for my child.

Tears

> *It is such a secret place, the land of tears.*
> Antoine de Saint-Exupéry

When our children weep, because they are sad or hurt or disappointed, we automatically say, "Honey, don't cry," in the hope of comforting them.

Perhaps we should think about what we're saying. Are we truly comforting them? Or are we giving them the message that tears are bad, that they should be hidden or wiped away?

It hurts us to see our children cry. But we hurt them more when we don't allow them to express their pain freely.

When our children know they can cry—and that we, too, sometimes cry—tears are less scary, less secretive. They're simply part of life.

Affirmation: Let me hold you while you cry.

Expectations

Parents see their children as bunches of potential.
   Pamela Espeland and Rosemary Wallner

Look at those fingers! When Johnnie grows up, he's going to be a concert pianist!

Maria takes after her mom, she's bound to be a beauty.

You can tell how smart Sasha already is by how fast he puts that puzzle together.

But what if Johnnie never plays the piano? Or Maria doesn't inherit her mother's looks? Or Sasha ends up an average student, more interested in football than physics?

It's great to want our children to excel, as long as we love them exactly as they are. How they turn out tomorrow and the next day and the next depends a great deal on how thoroughly we accept them right now, today.

Affirmation: I won't pressure my child.

Honesty

When in doubt, tell the truth.
Mark Twain

"I don't know" are three of the toughest words for parents to say. We want to have the answers. We want our children to feel secure that we know what we're doing, that they can depend on us at all times.

But sometimes we don't have the answers. "Why are some people wealthy and others homeless?" "Will I get chosen for the school play?" "Why did Grandpa have to die?"

"I don't know" is a perfectly good response. It tells our children two important things: that even grown-ups sometimes have uncertainty and doubts; and that telling the truth means acknowledging life's complex questions and enduring mysteries, which ultimately fosters greater security than fudging just so that we sound like we know what we're talking about.

Affirmation: I don't know.

A Day in the Life

Your four-year-old is invited to a birthday party at McDonald's. But you and your husband are strict vegetarians. Do you let your daughter eat a hamburger just this once? Or do you pack her off with a bag lunch of brown rice and tofu?

There is no right answer for this dilemma.

What you do depends on how you weigh your beliefs about diet with other aspects of your daughter's best interests.

Like many parenting questions, this situation begs a larger issue. In the years to come there will be many birthday parties and other events where your child will be exposed to values different from your own; will you insist on rigid adherence or will you encourage the "when in Rome" way of looking at things?

Moderation is helpful here. Principles are an important part of parenting. But so is sensitivity to your child's need to belong. Both must be well considered.

Affirmation: I'll use situational ethics.

Arguing

We never quarreled in front of the children.
Jehan Sadat

Although constant fighting between parents is alarming and damaging to children, there's nothing wrong with an occasional disagreement. Moms and dads often have differing opinions—on discipline, diet, and lots of other things—and when we do, it's better to work them out than to put on a false united front.

In fact it's healthy for kids to watch parents negotiate differences, as long as we're respectful of each other's opinions. Even when there's a bit of anger expressed, it's important to know that we can argue in the family without causing irreparable harm or losing one another's love.

Affirmation: Parents don't always have to agree.

Patience

Nagging is the repetition of unpalatable truths.
Baroness Edith Summerskill

A recent survey revealed that the number-one complaint of mothers is nagging. Moms hate being nagged. And we hate nagging our children. It's a grinding battle of wills with no side the victor.

So why is nagging such a prevalent part of parenting? Why can't we ask once, "Please pick up your toys," without repeating it over and over? Why can't "Mommy, can I have a cookie?" be satisfied with a simple yes-or-no answer?

Nagging wears us down, whether we're on the giving or the receiving end. Yet we all do it. Why? Moms and kids nag for exactly the same reason: because we want something and don't know any other way to get it.

Perhaps there *is* a better way. Maybe we need to stop—each time we start to nag or be nagged—and say to ourselves:

Affirmation: This isn't working. Let me ask—or answer—in a calmer, more productive way.

Lessons

Telling lies and showing off to get attention are the mistakes I made that I don't want my kids to make.
                    Jane Fonda

It takes courage to admit the mistakes we've made. But it's impossible to stop our children from repeating them.

We don't have the power to prevent it. We can be role models—positive examples of right and wrong—but we can't ensure that our children won't follow in our former footsteps. They have their own path to tread; the mistakes they make will be powerful, necessary life lessons, even if they're exactly the same ones we made years ago.

We can share what we've learned. Point out the pitfalls. But we can't expect our children to improve upon our past.

Affirmation: My children need to learn their own lessons.

Influence

God lends you your children until they're about eighteen years old. If you haven't made your points with them by then, it's too late.

Betty Ford

Actually our children are always on loan, whether they're eight, eighteen, or twenty-eight. They belong to themselves; on temporary loan for a brief period of time to be cuddled, counseled, loved, and cared for to the best of our ability.

As the famous poet Kahlil Gibran said, "They come through you but not from you, And though they are with you, yet they belong not to you."

Still, our influence lingers long after our children leave us. What they gain during their stay lasts throughout every single day of their lives.

Affirmation: I have guardianship, not ownership, of my child.

Delegation

> *When your schedule leaves you brain dead and stressed to exhaustion, it's time to delegate. Say no. Be brutal.*
> *Marilyn Ruman*

Motherhood adds an extra layer of stress to our already overscheduled lives. Whether we're home full-time or balancing career and children, the pressures mount; it's impossible to add one more item to our "to do" list without it exacting a cost.

Yet we find it so hard to say no. We're afraid of disappointing other people. We want to be liked. And after all, what's one more errand, one more favor, when we're already going full-tilt?

What we don't realize is that learning to say no is a way of saying yes. Yes to protecting our limited time and energy. Yes to our health and well-being. Yes to our sanity so that we can concentrate on what's really important, on what really matters the most.

Affirmation: I'll say yes to myself.

Expression

Nobody has ever measured, not even poets, how much the heart can hold.

Zelda Fitzgerald

How do we quantify the overwhelming joy, gratitude, and passionate protectiveness our children inspire?

We measure our affection in smiles that radiate at the sight of our child.

We measure it in tears that flow when we are flooded with tenderness.

We measure it in pride that swells us until we feel as if we will burst with love—our hearts holding more than we ever imagined possible.

Affirmation: My love is boundless.

Lovemaking

Six weeks after Ben's birth my obstetrician declared me ready to resume sexual relations. Whatever that meant.
  Roberta Israeloff

The idea of sex after childbirth may be exciting, a dreaded inevitability, or anything in between.

For many new moms, resuming making love is a smooth transition and much-needed source of pleasure and nourishment.

But if you're not ready—for reasons of exhaustion, discomfort, or just because frankly it's the farthest thing from your mind—just say not yet. Be honest. Ask your mate to be patient. Desire will return. Sooner or later making love will seem like a welcome idea.

Affirmation: I'll give myself as much time as I need.

Realism

You become about as exciting as your food blender. The kids come in, look you right in the eye, and ask if anybody's home.

Erma Bombeck

Our children only see us in relation to themselves; we are their lifeline, their sustenance, their mother.

Yet we are much more than mothers. And it's important for our children to see the other aspects of our lives that make us who we are.

There are many ways to give our children a more realistic, full picture of us as whole, separate individuals, both at home and out in the world. We can take them to see where we work; we can bring them along to exercise class or to a political rally; we can show them pictures from high school, college, or the day we were married.

The more they see us separate from themselves, the less likely they are to take our mothering for granted.

Affirmation: I'm a mother and much, much more.

Expertise

> *I really learned it all from mothers.*
> Dr. Benjamin Spock

An incredibly significant tribute from the most famous child-raising expert of all time.

It's good to remember that although we may not be "professionals"—we may never give a seminar or write a book—when it comes to our children, we're the real experts.

We can—and should—seek advice. But ultimately it's the everyday, hands-on experience that gives us the wisdom and knowledge we need.

Affirmation: I know my child really, really well.

Expenses

I could now afford all the things I never had as a kid, if I didn't have kids.

Robert Orben

I've met lots of women in their late twenties and early thirties who are hesitant to take on the financial burden of parenthood. "I've worked so hard to make it," they say. "Why blow it all on diapers, strollers, not to mention the cost of a college education?"

Yet ask any mother, well-off or struggling, and she'll undoubtedly say that having a child is worth way more than it costs. We make sacrifices, deny ourselves luxuries (and sometimes necessities as well), yet what we're given in return enriches our lives beyond measure.

Affirmation: It's worth every dime.

Authority

Because I said so.

> *All mothers*

Before I was a mother, I vowed I'd never—never—resort to giving my children this lame excuse for an answer.

I confess. Now that I am a mother, I use it. Sparingly. And believe it or not, sometimes it's the very best answer of all. It's short. It's conclusive. And it prevents a forty-five-minute discussion when a simple no will do. And it's true.

Every question doesn't warrant a summit meeting. When the real answer is "Because I said so," why not say so? Sometimes kids are just glad to know who's in charge.

Affirmation: I'm in charge.

Consequences

Remember when your mother used to say: "Go to your room"? Now a kid goes to his room and he's got an air conditioner, a TV set, an intercom, a shortwave radio. . . .
Sam Levenson

Good point! Maybe it's time to rethink our idea of what constitutes "punishment."

Banishing our child to his room, where he's free to play electronic games, watch TV, or talk on the phone, is hardly an effective form of discipline. Yet we often do just that.

It's important to make conscious disciplining decisions. Taking a toy away from a toddler, putting a three-year-old in her room to think about her behavior, or grounding a grade-schooler from the phone are all appropriate consequences. The kids may protest loudly, but that just means we're making our point. We must do what's ultimately best for our children, not what's easiest on ourselves.

Affirmation: I carefully think through consequences.

Ungratefulness

> *There are times when parenthood seems nothing but feeding the hand that bites you.*
>
> *Peter De Vries*

Little is more infuriating than when children are ungrateful. When they complain that the game—the one we went to four different toy stores in search of—is *not* the one they saw on TV. When they argue over which video to rent. When they forget to say "thank you" after you produce exactly the giant-chocolate-chip-cookie birthday cake they begged for.

At these times we wonder if our attempts at teaching manners are for naught. We have to bite our tongue for fear of blurting out that age-old parenting line: "You're complaining and meanwhile there are children who are starving."

And at these times we need to remember who we are dealing with. Children. No better, no worse than any other children. With time they will learn to be gracious, to say "thank you," without us saying a word.

Affirmation: Give it time.

Grocery-shopping

I was doing the family grocery-shopping accompanied by two children, an event I hope to see included in the Olympics in the near future.

Anna Quindlen

Now, this is an act of infinite courage and stamina! It takes strategy, determination, and twice as much time as it did back when we had the luxury of grocery-shopping solo.

If taking kids with you is your only option, here are a few helpful dos and don'ts:

- DO bring a list. Don't veer off course even if they beg for Froot Loops and Tootsie Rolls.
- DON'T shop anywhere where you have to bag your own groceries. What you gain in savings you lose in sanity.
- DO buy something early on that they can eat in the cart.
- DON'T plan anything else to do that day; you'll be exhausted by the time you're finished.
- DO change diapers or insist on potty tries *before* you go. It's not surefire, but it increases your odds of success.

Affirmation: I deserve a medal!

Control

> *If his eyes are wide open staring at a light, it does not mean*
> *he will not be asleep within minutes.*
> *Lydia Davis*

Second-guessing naptime is the primary sporting event of early motherhood. Such suspense! Will she or won't she go down for an afternoon nap? Will it be long enough to shower and return calls, or should I make the calls first, or should I take the cellular phone into the shower, in which case will I get electrocuted? If I let her sleep more than an hour (Ah, a blessed hour!), will I pay for it later tonight when I *really* need a break?

Ironically the more we try to control naptimes—manipulating schedules, wishing and hoping (and praying) they'll sleep—the more tense we get. It reminds me of the saying A watched pot never boils. When she's ready to sleep, she's ready, and not a moment before.

Affirmation: I can't control my child's schedule.

Intelligence

Every child is born a genius.
         R. Buckminster Fuller

Certainly Buckminster Fuller didn't mean that every child comes into the world with a staggering IQ and the potential to win the Nobel Prize.

More likely he speaks to the native intelligence each of us possesses, which, if neglected, can be dulled or even extinguished.

How do we keep the spark alive? By reading to our children from the time they are born. By never talking down to them; rather, assuming they are capable of comprehending a thoughtful answer to any question they ask. By nurturing their creativity; by taking an active role in their education.

And by always—always—believing that:

Affirmation: My child is capable of greatness.

Innocence

> *I went to Macy's to see Santa Claus and listen to the kids; it was like a business convention at the Statler Hilton.*
> Richard Lindner

Our small children are full of wonder; they wait for the Tooth Fairy until their eyelids begin to droop; are mesmerized by the lights of the menorah, nod knowingly at the empty plate of cookies Santa consumed before dashing off to his next destination.

Yet eventually all children wise up. They write notes to the Tooth Fairy and remind *us* to make sure to look under the pillow. They negotiate with Santa, knowing full well he's just a man with a red suit and a big white beard hired by the department store.

Does this make our children materialistic? Cynical? Corrupt? Hardly. It's just part of growing up. Still it makes us yearn for the time when they were more innocent, when they believed in it all.

Affirmation: My child's innocence is precious as long as it lasts.

Gift Giving

Whaddya bring me?
> *All kids*

My mother-in-law, Jane, always thought this would be the perfect name for a gift shop, preferably located in airports, where parents and grandparents could load up on presents for their kids.

Since I travel often, trip gifts (otherwise known as guilt gifts) have come to be expected by my children, an agreed-upon ransom for my being away. My friend, Susan, a corporate vice president who travels several times a month, cautioned me against this, saying, "When my kids started asking when I was leaving, I started cutting back on the gifts."

It's great to bring back presents, mementos, something small, as long as our children don't associate our leaving with hitting the jackpot. As long as they're happy to see us—not just happy to see what we bring.

Affirmation: Modest gifts mean just as much.

A Day in the Life

You're going up the escalator at the mall with your one-year-old in tow, when you notice another mom screaming at her dawdling toddler, "Get going or I'll never take you anywhere again!" You recoil as she grabs the back of his neck and smacks him across the behind. You want to say something. You open your mouth, and then you stop, the words caught in the back of your throat. What's the right thing to do?

This is a wrenching ethical call, one that each of us struggles with whenever we witness an incident of child abuse.

We want to speak up, but we're scared, and for good reason. What right have we to judge another parent? What if saying something backfires, resulting in further hurt to the child? What if we end up in a screaming match with a stranger in the middle of a crowd?

Sadly nearly everyone finds himself or herself in this situation. Each time, we need to ask ourselves this question: *Is there something I can do to help?* If the answer is yes, then be sure to intervene carefully and with compassion.

Affirmation: We are all responsible for the safety of children.

Privacy

Respect the child. Trespass not on his solitude.
Ralph Waldo Emerson

When our children are small, they want nothing more than to be in our company twenty-four hours a day. Then, little by little, they begin to assert their independence. They shut the bathroom door. They want privacy with their friends. We ask, "What did you do in school today?" and they say, "Nothing," when we know full well they are choosing not to divulge the details of their day.

This is a significant shift in parenting. We're used to being privy to their every movement; we're surprised— and perhaps even feel shut out—when they want to be alone.

Yet they have every right to their solitude and their space. Their private thoughts, dreams, conversations, are just that—private. And deserving of respect.

Affirmation: I'll honor my child's need for privacy.

Choices

> *I don't care what Andy's mother lets him do.*
> *All mothers*

Here we go again, uttering exactly the same words that frustrated us so when our own mother (and her mother, and her mother . . .) said them to us.

We say them because they're true. Little did we know just how true they were. Andy's mother may let him eat Pop-Tarts for breakfast, but that doesn't mean we're about to throw our nutritional guidelines out the window. So what if Susie's mother lets her ride her tricycle without a helmet? Or Gwen's father lets her stay up past nine?

We learn quickly that there are lots of different ways of parenting. We must make choices in our own child's interest without feeling pressured or pushed to be like anyone else on the block.

Affirmation: I don't have to live up to anyone else's standards but my own.

Contributions

One hesitates to bring a child into this world without fixing it up a little.

Alta

As parents, we have a responsibility to "fix up" our world in whatever ways we can: by organizing neighborhood crime protection, by helping the homeless, by working to create a healthier environment.

When we do our part, we achieve two important goals: 1. We make a difference. 2. We set an example to our children of the importance of taking an active role in contributing to our community.

We don't have to change the world; we simply have to do our small part. For our children's sake and for all children's sake.

Affirmation: I can make a difference.

Emotional Security

> *The future of the world would be assured if every child was loved.*
>
> Dr. Bernie Siegel

What a difference it would make if every child felt secure, their physical and emotional needs consistently met by a devoted, loving parent. Apathy. Violence. Everything from garden-variety rudeness to serious crime might be lessened, even obliterated if our world was filled with a generation of human beings who truly felt loved.

This may sound like a utopian vision, impossible to attain. But as the Talmudic saying goes, Save one soul and it is as if you've saved the entire world.

Affirmation: I'm helping secure the future.

"Working Mothers"

Working mothers often feel poised between the cultures of the housewife and the working man.
        Arlie Hochchild

Those of us combining career and motherhood continue to feel culturally alienated; we miss out on the morning playgroups and over-the-fence camaraderie shared by stay-at-home moms, and we aren't card-carrying members of the fast-track male-executive club either.

The goal isn't to fit in, but rather to design a new culture reflective of our emerging identity as mothers and careerwomen. We do this by forming support networks with other mothers in the workplace, by rejecting the idea of a "mommy track," by advocating for flexible hours and on-site child care, and by repeating to ourselves:

Affirmation: I'm carving out a new course.

Savings

> *Blessed are the young, for they shall inherit the national debt.*
> *Herbert Hoover*

In the nineties—as in the thirties—it's easy to feel discouraged about our children's financial security. Will we be able to send them to college? Will they have the financial resources to buy a home someday? Will Social Security be obsolete by the time they're old enough to qualify?

It's never too soon to start saving. Filling up a piggy bank when they're little; opening a bank account in their name; putting money away in an IRA or other long-term investments are all sound financial planning.

It doesn't have to be a lot. Anything we put away now helps our children bank on a secure financial future.

Affirmation: Every penny counts.

Quality Time

The best inheritance a parent can give his child is a few minutes of time each day.
O. A. Battista

More than a few minutes is preferable. But some days even the minimum requires juggling and putting other important things on hold.

But whether it's fifteen minutes or three full hours, what matters just as much is how the time is spent. Is it really quality time—time spent attending to them, undistracted, without a million other thoughts shooting through our brain? Are they getting our best attention? Or are we only half there—being in the same room while we're folding laundry, answering the phone, or trying to get dinner on the table?

We all have so much to do, it's hard to stop everything and *just* be with our children. But it's worth it. When we give them our time, we give them something terribly valuable—the feeling that, for at least these few minutes, they're the most important person of all.

Affirmation: How much time have I spent with my child today?

Slowing Down

It can take practice for adults to change over every so often to Children's Standard Time.
   Mr. Rogers and Barry Head

Mothers are perennially rushing. And in our rush, we get impatient with our children's dawdling; when it takes a full half hour to find their shoes and get them on; when they spend fifteen minutes staring at (and dissecting) a handful of dandelions when we're trying to get their jacket on and maneuver them out the door. And of course these inevitable childhood scenarios are most likely to occur when we're desperate to get them into the car and to daycare in order to get to our nine A.M. meeting on time.

Some things are urgent, others aren't. If there's truly no leeway, then we have to do whatever it takes to stay on schedule, even it means hurrying them along. But where we have some flexibility, we can try to adjust to Children's Standard Time. It's slower, dreamier, and a nice break from the hard deadlines of adulthood.

Affirmation: It's nice to slow down once in a while.

Obedience

This year we've decided to send the dogs to camp and the kids to obedience school.

Anonymous

But seriously, folks, obedience is a big issue. Do we expect our children to obey us simply because we're the parents? Or do we allow them to challenge every single thing we say?

Neither is effective. We need a balance, sometimes insisting our children follow the rules, other times being open to negotiation.

Many situations do require simple obedience: Going to bed without arguing, picking up toys, being reasonably considerate to siblings, taking orders in the face of danger.

Obedience is important to being civilized and vital to being safe. On the other hand, we don't want subservience. If there's a good reason for what's being asked—which there usually is—share it. Explaining to kids why we want them to obey goes a long way toward enlisting cooperation.

Affirmation: I don't have to be heavy-handed.

Birds and Bees

> *Don't bother to discuss sex with children; they rarely have anything to add.*
>
> Fran Lebowitz

My friend Beth asked her seven-year-old son, Louis, if he knew what sex was. "Of course," he replied, "it's when grown-ups go upstairs and kiss and hug all night long!"

When is the right time to start talking to our kids about the facts of life?

The answer is simple: When they ask.

Which differs greatly among children. Some ask probing questions as early as three, others don't ask until close to puberty, and some never ask at all. (There are several good books on the subject, including my personal favorite, *Where Do Babies Come From?*)

There are many points at which we can introduce information, but we needn't be proactive on the subject before the kids are approaching puberty. Until then we can relax. When they're ready, we just need to follow their lead.

Affirmation: Timing is everything.

A Day in the Life

Your son just celebrated his first birthday, and life is slowly getting back to normal. He's sleeping through the night, you've lost the weight you gained in pregnancy, and you and your husband have started to have a romantic relationship again. What's wrong with this picture? Nothing, except the tiny voice in your head that keeps saying, "Time to have another baby." Or is it?

It happens to almost everyone.

Unless you're certain that you want only one child, the "Should we or shouldn't we?" question typically comes up right around the first birthday, just when life seems finally to be settling down.

There are definite pros and cons. Some people advocate for spacing kids closely, arguing that as long as you're already in baby mode, you may as well get on with it. And there's something to be said for siblings close in age; they can share toys, have mutual interests, and look after each other once they're in school.

On the con side there's the "diaper dilemma." Many parents wait until the older child is out of diapers, feeling overwhelmed at the idea of two toddlers wreaking havoc in unison. Plus, many experts agree that sibling rivalry is diminished with a few years in between.

There is no right answer. But whether sooner or later, a second child creates both upheaval and joy.

Affirmation: This is just as big a decision the second time around.

Education

> *A child educated only at school is an uneducated child.*
> George Santayana

In the beginning we are our children's primary teachers. Everything they learn they learn directly from us: how to drink from a cup, how to count from one to ten and recite the letters of the alphabet, how to put one foot in front of the other without falling over in a heap.

Then we send our children off to nursery school, to kindergarten, first grade, and all the way up to college, gradually putting their education in other people's hands.

This is a mistake. No matter how old our children are, we need to be in partnership with their educators. Advocating on their behalf when necessary. Supplementing what they learn at school with what we teach them at home. Nurturing their intellectual development by pointing out the "lessons" present in everyday life.

Affirmation: I play a vital role in my child's education.

Tantrums

A mere parent pitted against a child in a test of wills in a toy store is a terrible spectacle.
George F. Will

Tantrums. There's only one thing worse for parents, and that's tantrums in public, where the whole world can witness our children at their worst.

Most parents experience this nightmare sooner or later, especially during the "terrible twos." It usually occurs in crowded places—in the grocery store checkout line, in the middle of a department store, at church or synagogue services, just as the hymn ends and the sermon starts.

So what's a parent to do in the face of a screaming, hysterical child who's flung herself on the floor?

First, stay calm. Look as if you've barely noticed. In your most matter-of-fact tone of voice instruct your child to get up, *or* if you must, pick her up and remove her from the premises. If this isn't possible, simply ignore the scene while you finish your business, then proceed as directed.

Second, don't negotiate. It's a sign of weakness, and besides, it won't work.

Third, remember, this, too, shall pass. Unless your child has serious behavioral problems, tantrums are a stage most kids grow out of by the time they're four or five.

Affirmation: Staying calm will help me get through this.

Separation

> *There is no fear as great in a small child as that of being left alone.*
>
> T. Berry Brazelton

We eagerly await the baby-sitter's arrival, give her detailed instructions, kiss the baby good-bye, and then are completely undone as she bursts into inconsolable sobs, reaching for us as if she's been abandoned forever.

It's so, so hard to leave when our children are crying. Whether they're eighteen months and suffering separation anxiety or six years old, afraid of going to bed without us at their side, it makes us feel so guilty and worried, it's almost not worth it to go.

But go we must. Even if it means leaving with a heavy heart. I used to literally push myself out the door with Zoe's screams echoing behind me, drive two blocks to the Park Kwik, and call the baby-sitter to make sure the crying had stopped. (Ironically it often had; it takes our leaving for them to finally settle down.)

Meanwhile how can we make it easier on our children and on ourselves? Call home if it reassures you. Leave a comfort object or create a special sign (I still kiss my children on a certain place that they can "rub" while I'm away; I know another couple who left their daughter a video of themselves when they went on vacation).

Little by little, over time and with experience, our children come to trust that we return.

Affirmation: I'll always come back.

Authority

No matter how much kids resent authority, they resent even more being left with none at all.
        Art Linkletter

So many of us go into parenting thinking we'll be friends with our children. Perhaps we resented our parents' authority or felt—even as young adults—that we didn't have a voice. So we bend over backward giving our children freedom, forgetting that they also need structure and authority in order to feel secure.

Seeing parents firmly take charge makes kids feel safe. As one six-year-old put it, "Moms and dads are 'sposed to know what to do so they can tell me what I'm 'sposed to do."

Being in charge doesn't make us dictators; it simply gives kids rules and boundaries so as not to be overwhelmed by a world much too big and much too complex for them to find their way in all alone.

Affirmation: Authority is a form of love.

Guilt

> *When your child has a difficult time, it's only natural to think, "What did I do wrong?"*
> Nancy Reagan

This is universally true for mothers. Our son wets his bed until he's six, and we assume it's because of all the time spent in day care; our daughter doesn't get invited to a neighbor's birthday party, and we figure it's because we weren't friendly enough to her mother; our child does poorly in school, and we blame it on our marital problems.

Interestingly it doesn't work in reverse. When our kids do something fabulous, we don't take credit and congratulate ourselves. Yet when they struggle or fail, we assume we must have damaged them somewhere along the way.

The truth is we are seldom culpable for causing our children's difficulties. And taking them on isn't productive. We can help them do better, we can sympathize with them and support them, but their trials and their triumphs are their own.

Affirmation: What did I do right?

Dependence

*My obstetrician was so dumb that when I gave birth, he forgot
to cut the cord. For a year that kid followed me everywhere.*
Joan Rivers

When they're little, it's almost as if they're attached at
the hip. Our small children do follow us everywhere—
hanging on our arm while we're trying to talk on the
phone, nipping at our heels wherever we go, wanting to
be in our lap even when we go to the bathroom.

When you've simply got to have some space, either
because your arms are full of groceries, there's someone at
the door, or *just* because you need some solitude, the old
standards work best: An infant swing is one safe diversion-
ary tactic; a playpen is another; a walker (unless you're
opposed for what some consider safety reasons) is a third.

At times it's a drag to be pulled on constantly. But the
good news is that gradually children do pull away, until
finally you're lucky if you can get them to stay in the
same room with you for more than a few minutes at a
time.

It may be hard to conceive of now, but enjoy their
company while you can.

Affirmation: I'll give myself a little space.

Influence

> *There was a time when Mrs. Einstein knew a lot more than Albert.*
>
> Marguerite Kelly

Or, for a variation on the old saying, Behind every great man there's a great mother.

No matter how brilliantly our children achieve, how far they go in the world, it's important to remember that our impact in large part lays the foundation for their future accomplishments.

Everything we do right now—feeding them, cuddling them, reading to them—is one of the building blocks that help them climb the ladder of success.

Affirmation: I take credit for all my positive influence.

Gratitude

Only when you become a father will you learn how to be a son.

Spanish proverb

In becoming parents we learn to be better sons and daughters. We realize how much our parents sacrificed to make a home, to provide the necessities, let alone the luxuries. We understand their fears, their struggles, the countless ways they set aside their needs in order to provide for ours.

And we realize how much they must have loved us. As we gaze upon our own child, feeling our intense love and devotion, we look back at our parents through new eyes.

Affirmation: Now I understand.

Manners

> *The hardest job kids face today is learning good manners without seeing any.*
>
> Fred Astaire

We want our children to have good manners, but too often we forget to set good examples. A simple "please" when we ask our kids to pick up their toys. A "thank you very much" when they cooperate. Waiting our turn in line at the movie theater, not littering, helping an older person carry groceries out to her car, can be ways of modeling the respect we want our children to learn.

It's easy to forget. In all the stress of everyday life we sometimes issue orders rather than requests and are rude —or simply oblivious—to strangers; in short are less than considerate ourselves.

Yet if we are truly committed to manners, we need to show as well as tell, treating our children—and others— with utmost consideration and respect.

Affirmation: A positive example is the best teacher.

Listening

Even though I can't solve your problems, I will be there as your listening board whenever you need me.
Sandra K. Lamberson

We want to solve any and all difficulties our children face, but we can't. It's up to them to find creative solutions, whether it's our newborn figuring out how to roll over, our three-year-old learning to share, or our six-year-old working out problems with a playmate.

What we *can* do is be there for our children with open arms, sympathetic ears, and always the reassurance that, as their parent, we will do everything in our power to help.

Affirmation: I'm here if you need me.

Supermom

> *Mothers are people who fold over your peanut butter sandwich for you.*
>
> Robert Paul Smith

For Evan's fourth birthday party I spent an hour and a half methodically cutting crusts off twenty-four slices of Wonder bread to make cookie-cuttered peanut-butter-and-jelly sandwiches. At Zoe's fifth birthday I served rice cakes decorated as clowns with shredded carrot hair, raisin eyes, and gumdrop noses perfectly placed in the center of each face.

Over the years I've calmed down considerably. The past several parties have featured take-out pizza; this year I really wised up and invited the kids to come at three in the afternoon and got away with just cupcakes and milk.

Did they care? Of course not. Did I? Not once I realized that being a good mother doesn't require such herculean efforts. Sometimes the simpler the better.

Affirmation: I don't have to win "Mother of the Year."

Self-actualization

To be a really good, creative mother you have to be an extraordinary woman.

Meryl Streep

Although millions of women do it, there's nothing ordinary at all about what it takes to be a mother. Patience. Ingenuity. Creativity. The capacity for love in great measure. These are only a few of the qualifications for this extraordinary vocation.

But in order to *be* an extraordinary mother, we need to be *more* than a mother. We need to be a well-rounded individual, constantly developing our talents, honing our skills, deepening our spirituality, growing all the time, just as our children continue to grow.

Affirmation: I am growing as a mother and as a person.

Rebelliousness

> *Cosby's First Law of Intergenerational Perversity: no matter what you tell your child to do he will always do the opposite.*
> Bill Cosby

Is this because children are innately contrary? Do they automatically go against our wishes in order to aggravate us? Do they take perverse pleasure in giving us a hard time? In other words do they say no just because we want them to say yes?

Sometimes. When kids are resistant, it may be their way of asserting independence and expressing their own unique point of view.

When they appear to be difficult, just for the sake of it, it helps to remember how little power they really have. Two strategies: Give them as much say as possible about as many things as you can; and avoid giving them *more* power by engaging in the battle.

Affirmation: I don't have to overreact.

Sickness

When your child is sick, all perspective slides into the ocean.
Liz Rosenberg

When mothers say, "I wish it were me instead of you," we really mean it. There's nothing more miserable than sitting helplessly by as our children wheeze and cough, moan with the stomach flu, or nurse a broken collarbone. We'd do anything—anything—to ease their pains.

Yet all we can do is attempt to comfort them, by feeding them soup, reading stories, placing a cool hand on their fevered brow.

It's frightening when our children are sick. It reminds us how fragile they are and makes us immensely grateful once they are back to their healthy, vigorous selves.

Affirmation: My child will be better soon.

Priorities

> *For a while I was convinced that parenthood equals socks.*
> Phil Donahue

We get all wrapped up in the more mundane aspects of parenting; sometimes entire days go by where it's all maintenance and precious little meaningful connection.

Then we have to make an extra effort. By taking time to play with our children even if a pile of dirty socks waits another day. By spending uninterrupted time talking, reading together, taking walks, baking cookies, listening to music—anything that brings us closer together.

Socks can wait. Or be replaced. But the time we fail to spend with our children can never be recovered.

Affirmation: I'll try to remember what's most important.

Responsibility

The children always helped their mother to edit my books.
Mark Twain

Children love to have a hand in helping parents work, whether it's stirring the soup, sorting the mail, or pushing Return on the computer, as my son, Evan, used to do in order to help me write my books.

Giving kids a "job" is good for two reasons: it's empowering for them to take responsibility; and it's a way of letting them participate in the daily details of our lives.

Even very small children can make a contribution if we give them the chance. And you know what? It's great to have them on our team.

Affirmation: Every little bit helps.

Tolerance

> *Families with babies and families without babies are sorry for each other.*
>
> Edgar Watson Howe

As I'm nearing forty, I've met more and more people who've chosen not to have children. People who say, "I just don't have the patience," or "I wouldn't want so much responsibility," or "I work hard and I love the freedom. I don't want to worry about supporting a family."

On the one hand I understand their position. Raising children is hard, time-consuming, and expensive. On the other hand as a mother it's hard to imagine life without children. It seems relatively empty and meaningless (although undoubtedly quieter).

In fact both having children and remaining child-free are legitimate choices. Both involve trade-offs and differing rewards. Both deserve understanding and acceptance.

Affirmation: I'm happy with my choice.

Real Life

We want our children to have picture-perfect lives.
Harriet Hodgson

All parents start out with the dream that our children
will have "perfect lives." That they'll never suffer bruises,
endure disappointments, or face failure. Not if *we* we can
help it.

Gradually we come to our senses. We accept—even
embrace—the fact that "perfect" is a fantasy and not
necessarily the goal. What's more ideal is for our children
to have rich, full lives, including inevitable ups and downs
—and to develop the strength to learn from whatever
comes their way.

Affirmation: I give up my illusions.

A Day in the Life

Your neighbor, a mother of two, reads you the riot act when you give in and give your toddler the cookie he's been screaming for over the past half hour. "Isn't he a little spoiled?" she asks. What are you supposed to say?

Here's what you say: "Thanks, but it's really up to me to be the judge of that."

If that sounds harsh, it's far more polite than her unsolicited assessment of your parenting. Frankly whether you give your son the cookie or not is none of her business; every mother makes the best decisions she can, and the last thing you need is anyone's criticism.

Of course she may be right, although her delivery is bound to make you defensive. If you can get beyond your ire, you may want to consider her comment, deciding for yourself whether or not her point is well taken.

Whether she's right or not, you needn't put up with anyone's harsh judgments. What we all need is support for being the best mothers we know how to be.

Affirmation: Each of us is doing our best.

Honesty

Why do you make everything seem so wonderful when it isn't?

Zoe Stern

For example, Zoe goes on to say in her book, "when parents say, 'Everything's fine,' but they have that 'it's not fine' look on their face. Or, at the doctor's when parents say, 'That won't hurt a bit,' and then OWWW! and you feel like they lied to you."

What Zoe and other kids don't understand is how hard it is to know when to protect our children and when to prepare them for potential pain. We don't want them to be hurt, but we don't want to deceive them either.

As in most things, honesty is the best policy. Telling our kids the truth—and reassuring them that we'll help them through the hard times—is ultimately more loving than pretending everything will be all right.

Affirmation: I'll try to be honest.

Values

> *Parents owe their children a set of decent standards and solid*
> *moral values around which to build a life.*
> *Ann Landers*

Which of course begs the question: What *are* decent standards? The morals, ethics, and values we want to instill require our own deep introspection as we raise our children.

Our values are constantly evolving, in many cases becoming more conservative as we go. Perhaps we experimented with sex or drugs, hitchhiked through Europe, rode a motorcycle, but the idea of our kids doing the same makes us shudder and quake.

What we believed at twenty is different from what we believe at thirty and forty; having children changes the equation that much more.

Here's an interesting research result from experts in child development: Kids who avoid the worst problems—drug abuse, teen pregnancy, and the like—are often kids whose parents taught them *values,* regardless of *what* those parental values were.

Affirmation: My values are the right ones to teach my children.

TV: The Third Parent.
      R. Buckminster Fuller

How much TV? What kind of programming is appropriate and what should be censored? Is violence really a problem? Should television be used as a baby-sitter? As a reward? If so, in what situations?

These are issues our grandparents didn't have to deal with. Yet today television is a constant presence, with some thirty-five channels available through network and cable. Some parents welcome it as an educational tool and a great way to get a break; others perceive it as an insidious interruption and competition to other, more worthwhile family activities.

Wherever you fall in the spectrum, here's an experiment to try: For the next two days unplug the television and see what happens. You will probably find yourself choosing more discriminately—and less often—to turn it back on.

Affirmation: I'll monitor what—and how much—television my child watches.

Criticism

> *Do not join encounter groups. If you enjoy being made to feel*
> *inadequate, call your mother.*
> Liz Smith

At first read I found this quote terribly insulting. How dare humorist Liz Smith even facetiously imply that mothers make their children feel bad about themselves?

After calming down I've decided there's some truth to what she says. Not out of malice, not out of meanness, mothers *do* tend to be critical of their children. We have such high hopes and are so sensitive to their every flaw. Inadvertently our well-meaning advice can come across as judgment; our desire to help our children can make them feel as if they can't possibly please us enough.

Yet it isn't our children's job to make us happy. Rather it is up to us to accept and affirm their efforts, even when they fall short of our expectations.

Affirmation: I'll watch my tendency to be critical.

Preparation

Always be prepared.
> *The Girl Scout's Motto*

This could just as easily be the Mother's Motto.

Always be prepared for your baby to fall asleep right as you get into the car. Always be prepared for your two-year-old to fill her diaper the minute after you give up and remove her from the potty chair. Always be prepared for your three-year-old to catch a bad cold right in the middle of your busiest time at work.

Always be prepared with extra pacifiers, Band-Aids, a list of backup sitters, and all the spare patience you can find. Because in case of an emergency—and there will be plenty—being prepared to regroup, revise, and improvise can make the difference between panic and peace of mind.

Affirmation: I'm prepared.

Eating Out

> *Children never want to eat in restaurants. What they want is*
> *to play under the table until the entrees arrive, then go to the*
> *bathroom.*
>
> *Dave Barry*

Taking small children to restaurants (and expecting a lovely, relaxing evening out) is one of the most unrealistic notions parents have. Unless they're newborns and happily captive in their infant seat, they're usually bored and we're usually disappointed and end up more worn out than when we started.

I can count on one hand the times I've managed it successfully. To be exact, three: once when there was a game room attached to the restaurant, once when a particularly nice waiter took the children for a tour of the kitchen, and once when a woman had a stroke and the paramedics came, which, heartless though it sounds, kept the kids' rapt attention until dessert arrived.

Most of the time it's a fiasco. We spend our entire meal shushing the children, begging them to stop making sugar-and-ketchup concoctions, going off on endless expeditions to the bathroom.

Eat at home. It's cheaper and a lot less trouble. Besides, it makes going out—and leaving the kids with a babysitter—that much more of a treat.

Affirmation: I won't make my children grow up before they're ready.

Inner Strength

A woman is like a tea bag; you don't know her strength until she's in hot water.

      Nancy Reagan

And you really don't know a *mother's* strength until her children are hurt or in any sort of danger.

Just witness a mother whose child has just fallen down at the park. One second she's calmly sitting on a bench reading a magazine, the next second she flies across the park like the Bionic Woman on a life-and-death mission.

The strength of mothers—especially when it comes to our children—is amazing to behold. We stay up four nights in a row, not even feeling our fatigue, as we nurse a sick child back to health. We fight like a lioness when someone threatens or treats our child unfairly. When our child is in need, we find courage and fortitude we didn't even know we possessed.

But we needn't wait for a crisis in order to know the extent of our inner strength. We should claim it and celebrate it every day, saying to ourselves:

Affirmation: I am incredibly strong.

Compassion

Let your children be more in awe of your kindness than your power.

George Savile

Kindness has a magical effect on children. And it goes a lot farther than exercising power.

There are lots of situations when we can choose compassion over castigation. Instead of reprimanding our child for acting out, we can hold him in our arms and say, "I can see that you need attention right now." Instead of yelling or punishing our child for hurting another child, we can gently say, "You must feel awfully lonely now that your friend no longer wants to play."

There's no need to rule with a heavy hand. Our children obey and respect us more when they see us as their allies.

Affirmation: I can rule with a soft touch.

Precociousness

Some of our modern children are so precocious, the birds and bees should study them.
Chester L. Marks

A major television event of 1991 was the children's program hosted by Magic Johnson, recently diagnosed HIV positive, during which he demonstrated the use of a condom.

Now, I don't know about you, but I felt pretty mixed watching my children watching Magic Johnson pull a balloon over the top of a banana. I understand the need for education. I know it's a tough world out there, in which some kids as young as eleven and twelve are sexually active.

On the other hand I cringe at the need for our children to be that aware, that fluent, that preoccupied with such adult matters. I wish they could be littler longer, more insulated for a few more years. Still, what I want most—and what most mothers want most—is for our children to be safe.

Affirmation: I want my child to grow up slowly.

A Day in the Life

Your two-and-a-half-year-old daughter finally did it! She went on the potty, and you're so excited, you're ready to bronze it and hang it on the mantel. The next day you try it again. No go. And the next day. And the next. You know she's ready, so why isn't she doing it? Should you bribe? Cajole? Take away her diapers?

Don't do anything. Making a huge deal out of toilet training is sure to backfire; nonchalance is a far better strategy.

There's no point pushing. All it will accomplish is to frustrate your child and frustrate yourself. Sooner or later, usually between ages two and three, the great majority of children toilet train themselves without any formal program or consistent reminders.

Having said all that, I've been told by lots of parents that bribery is often effective. Rewarding your child with a small token (one mother I knew had a "surprise bag" filled with toys that her child could pick from each time he went) may help and probably can't hurt.

Small rewards? Why not. Pressure? Never.

Affirmation: Everything in its own good time.

Solitude

A mother is someone who: looks forward to getting a root canal so she can sit quietly in one place.
Beth Mende Conne

A root canal? Well, maybe not. But most moms of small children will go to considerable lengths for a few hours of uninterrupted peace and quiet.

Two women in southern California banked on it: They opened "Moms Camp," a weekend getaway where harried mothers rest, relax, and are waited on hand and foot.

Luxurious, huh? Self-indulgent? Every single one of us deserves it. The problem is money and time.

For most of us Moms Camp is at best a wistful fantasy. Still, it's possible to find more affordable ways of temporarily retreating from parenting. A night off with friends, a drive in the country, even an hour alone just sitting by the window losing ourselves in a book can be incredibly restorative. We need it and we've earned it!

Affirmation: I'll savor the rare moments of solitude.

Conscience

> *The principal goal of parenting is to teach our children to become their own parents.*
> *Wayne Dyer*

Or, in Freudian terms, to develop in our children a healthy superego—the inner voice that legislates right from wrong and guides us in making responsible decisions. It is the voice that warns, *No, don't touch that stove, it's hot!* It's the voice that says, *If you tear up that picture book, you won't be able to read it anymore.* It's the voice that reminds, *If you're nice to people, they'll be nice in return.*

As children experience firsthand the consequences of their actions, the "parental voice" becomes internalized. Instead of hearing our voice, they hear their own.

Affirmation: My child is developing a sense of right and wrong.

Overprotectiveness

Q. *Were you worried your daughter would find out about the fire?*

A. *No. I took Beatrice right down and said, "That's Granny's castle. See how Daddy is helping put out the fire?"*

> *Interview between Diane Sawyer*
> *and Duchess "Fergie"*

Most of us don't have to deal with castles on fire and Daddy saving historic treasures from the flames. We *do* face much more common but equally tough situations: the death of a grandparent, the loss of a job, illness in the family, times when we need to decide how much to tell our children and to what degree to shield them from the truth.

More and more, parents today are choosing to be open and honest. We've learned that what children imagine is often scarier than what's real. With our help they can usually handle more than we think.

Affirmation: My child needn't be insulated from reality.

Rejoicing

Rejoice with your family in the beautiful land of life.
Albert Schweitzer

Beginning with the birth of our child, being a family offers abundant opportunities for rejoicing. Each birthday, each holiday, each time our child achieves another milestone is cause for celebration.

We needn't limit our festivities to standard holidays or life-cycle events. Some families create rituals all their own. For example, many years ago my friend Rhoda, her husband, and their two children instituted an annual ritual, a special time designated for each family member to share their positive achievements. I know another family who goes all out on May Day, complete with a May basket exchange and neighborhood parade.

Rejoicing together bonds us as a family—we look back and taste the laughter and the joy.

Affirmation: There's so much to celebrate.

Bathrooms

What it really means to be a parent is: you will spend an enormous portion of your time lurking outside public toilet stalls.

                    Dave Barry

Let's take a minute to talk about kids and public toilets.

This may not be a savory subject, but it's a reality for all parents, in need of serious debate. Take, for example, the changing tables in airport women's rooms. They're a terrific convenience, but why aren't they also in the men's rooms? What's a father traveling with an infant or toddler supposed to do?

And how about public facilities that don't allow boys over the age of two? Are moms supposed to let their young sons go into the bathroom unattended while they wait nervously outside?

I'm encouraged by an innovation I recently saw at the Minneapolis Mall of America: family restrooms. Everyone's welcome, no discrimination allowed. It's nonsexist and it's a lot safer.

Affirmation: Let's make all aspects of family life easier.

Pressure

> *I am certain that any child who does not take tap dancing and*
> *tennis lessons will end up in analysis.*
> Caryl Rivers and Alan Lupe

I'm assuming this is meant as a sarcastic comment on contemporary parents' need to push their children.

But *is* it pushing? Or are we merely trying to give our children every possible chance to develop their talents?

It depends on who we're doing it for. I was adamant that Zoe take up a musical instrument until I realized that her natural abilities lie elsewhere. "But it will be so much fun!" I told her, remembering my days of playing trumpet in the school band. I felt like such a good parent renting the flute, signing up for the six-private-lesson package, supervising her practice. Meanwhile she struggled to keep up, pressured and miserable.

Here's what I learned: Sampling most any kind of lessons is a good thing. But making a long-term commitment—whether it's gymnastics, piano, or kids' karate—is only good if our children are game.

Affirmation: My child doesn't have to be a star.

Confidences

Never trust anyone with a secret, except your mother.
Irene Zahava

We're tempted to reveal our children's confidences to others; often they're funny or poignant or just so sweet, we have trouble keeping them to ourselves.

But we mustn't. When our two-year-old tells us about his imaginary playmate ("Shhh! No one knows about him except you and me!"), when our five-year-old confides her secret wish to join the Cub Scouts, when our ten-year-old whispers the name of her first crush in our ear, we must resist the urge to spread the news.

Our children's confidence is a sacred trust; to deserve it, we must be sure it is not violated.

Affirmation: I'll keep it under lock and key.

Time Passing

> *I'm horrified by how quickly my children are growing.*
> Jonathan Lazear

Ditto. It is with a bittersweet mix of joy and sadness that we mark the passage of time. All too fast the soft, cuddly newborn turns into the dynamo toddler, who turns into the inquisitive schoolchild; we watch the "height lines" scrawled on the basement wall grow higher and higher and are amazed at how quickly the time went.

It may be impossible ever to imagine feeling this way as you hold your baby in your arms. But you will. In the meantime take every opportunity to document each passing stage. Take photographs, videos, keep a mother's journal describing your child at one, two, three . . . and every year along the way.

Affirmation: Every moment is precious.

Role Models

My mother and I go way back.
        Wendy Wasserstein

It can be scary to contemplate what a deep and lasting mark we leave on our children. Of all relationships the dynamic between mother and child has the most far-reaching influence; even once we're grown, we thank *and* blame our mothers for all the ways they affected us: "I trace my success to the fact that my mother always said I could do anything if I tried," or, "I'm still insecure because my mother never stopped criticizing how I looked."

We need to be aware of the messages we give our children. Because our words continue to ring in their ears long after they've ceased to hear our voice.

Affirmation: My child is listening.

Wholeness

> *Women's work is always toward wholeness.*
> May Sarton

Integration is another word for wholeness. The great challenge facing most mothers is how to integrate the various aspects of life—marriage, children, career, friendships, physical and spiritual fulfillment—into a working balance.

It's all too easy to neglect essential parts of ourselves, especially when our children are small; their needs are immediate (and often too loud) to ignore. So we focus on them, putting our own needs on hold.

It is only when we get sick or exhausted or intensely frustrated or away for a rare vacation that we notice our lives are out of balance. Days grow into weeks grow into months grow into years of self-neglect unless we break the pattern and put the pieces back together in a picture of wholeness.

Affirmation: All sides of me deserve attention.

Privacy

*The mother—poor invaded soul—finds even the bathroom
door no bar to hammering little hands.*
                    Charlotte Perkins Gilman

As I complete this book, I've noticed that bathrooms
pop up again and again on these pages. Maybe it's because
mothers spend an awful lot of time in the bathroom,
either keeping children company or trying to escape their
company for a few blissful moments of peace.

Here's my final word on the subject: *Lock the door.*
Unless you're worried that your child is in danger (playpens, swings, and walkers are meant for mother's bathroom breaks), you have every right to your privacy. This
is a basic example of setting limits, a way of saying,
"Right now I get to be alone." Because being a good
mother *doesn't* mean being at a child's constant beck and
call.

**Affirmation: Setting boundaries is a matter of self-
preservation.**

Worries

> *Considering how dangerous everything is, nothing is frightening.*
>
> Gertrude Stein

We can worry ourselves sick imagining all the terrible things that can happen to our child. What if she gets some terrible illness? What if something happens to my (or her father's) career and there's not enough money to support her? What if she's kidnapped? What if? What if? What if?

The world *is* dangerous, and awful things *do* happen. But we can't stop living because of fear. Rather we need to cultivate faith. Faith that our children will make it. Faith that we have the courage to steer through any storm.

Affirmation: I'll focus on what I can control, not on what I can't control.

PMS

*Women complain about premenstrual syndrome, but I think
of it as the only time of the month I can be myself.*
Roseanne Arnold

For those of us who experience PMS or "Sybilisque"
behavior before or during our menstrual period, that time
of the month presents an added mothering challenge.

How to be patient with children when we're crabby
and out of sorts? How to control outbursts and keep
things in perspective? How to stay focused on all our
responsibilities when we feel like crawling into bed and
hiding under the covers?

These are the times when we need to go easy on ourselves. Or when we need to get some extra time off. We
need to remember that being a good mother doesn't always mean being cheerful, even-tempered, and sweet.

Affirmation: I don't have to be a saint.

Reassurance

Piglet sidled up to Pooh from behind.
"Pooh," he whispered.
"Yes, Piglet?"
"Nothing," said Piglet, taking Pooh's paw, "I just wanted to be sure of you."
  A. A. Milne, The House at Pooh Corner

Sometimes our children need a little bit of extra reassurance. Their fingers wrap around us, simply wanting to feel our bigger hand encircling their own. They follow us from room to room keeping track of our whereabouts. They call out our name in the middle of the night just to make sure we're right where they can find us.

What do they want? Nothing in particular. And everything our presence represents: Security. Comfort. Love.

Affirmation: I'm right here.

Mornings

The trouble with dawn is that it comes too early in the day.
Susan Richman

Way too early and way too often, especially when our children are small and we've been up half the night.

For those of us who cherish their sleep (count me in), early mornings heralded by children's voices (usually eager and way too enthusiastic) are tough. Every little bit of sleep is a gift from God; we hit the snooze button and pray for another few minutes of blissful slumber before facing the day.

Some mothers actually grow to enjoy sunrise, while others say they never get used to its glare. In either case here are the two best pieces of advice I've heard on the subject: 1. Don't check the clock to calculate how long you've rested. 2. Wait fifteen minutes before deciding how you feel.

Affirmation: Good morning.

Toys

> *Toys are made in heaven, batteries are made in hell.*
> Tom Robbins

Those darn battery-operated toys. Inevitably our children unwrap birthday or holiday gifts only to discover they're missing the batteries. We're off to the hardware store faster than you can say Energizer, calling home to find out if they're double As or triple Bs.

Then there are those toys that require assembly, hours on our hands and knees putting pieces together. But the worst are the push toys. You know which ones I mean: the mechanical barking dog, the kiddie lawn mower, and the all-time-favorite vacuum cleaner with the rotating plastic balls guaranteed to give grown-ups a full-blown migraine.

Like so much else it's a stage. There are times kids just *have* to make noise. So it doesn't hurt to lay in a healthy supply of silent substitutes. Either books, anything Nerf, or a baby cassette player with headphones. (Okay, batteries are good for *some* things.)

Affirmation: Toys don't have to mean noise.

Affection

My mother was raised with a terror of touching, which left me feeling needy.

Mariette Hartley

One of my favorite bumper stickers is the one that reads "Have You Hugged Your Child Today?"

It always makes me think. *Have* I hugged my children today? Did I kiss them and cuddle them and ruffle their hair, or was I so busy and distracted that a day went by without being physically close?

Our children are very receptive to our affection when they are small. They crave it. They welcome it. I'm told as they grow older, they're less open to our physical advances, though they still come around for a cuddle every now and then. Which makes it terribly important to touch them a lot now, when they need it like water and air.

Affirmation: Have I hugged my child today?

Pressure

> *I'm thirty years old, but I read at the thirty-four-year-old level.*
>
> Dana Carvey

This sardonic quip from one of *Saturday Night Live*'s regulars reminds us not to panic about our children's development. It doesn't matter if they sit up at six months, read at six years, get their driver's license the moment they turn sixteen.

The most meaningful levels are those that our children naturally attain. Although some children have bona-fide learning disabilities and should have special help, we usually needn't worry when they aren't up to speed with the child-development charts. Instead we can watch for their individual progress. Start now by noticing one thing your child can do today that he couldn't do a week ago.

Affirmation: This week my child learned to

_____.

Little Things

Women are the glue that holds our day-to-day life together.
Anna Quindlen

Women, especially mothers, are the Super Glue that keeps so many things from coming apart. So much of what occupies our time and energy goes unnoticed, yet if *we* didn't do it, our family's quality of life would be severely diminished.

If we didn't go grocery-shopping, there might not be anything for dinner. If we didn't send out invitations, who would show up for the birthday parties? If we didn't make sure there were Band-Aids in the medicine cabinet, toilet paper in the pantry, advice whenever it's needed, our children wouldn't feel nearly so comfortable and secure.

We may call them the little things. But whatever we call them, like glue, what mothers give is invisible and indispensable.

Affirmation: Today I will notice all the "little things" I do for my family.

Priorities

Having it all doesn't necessarily mean having it all at once.
Stephanie Luetkehans

You've likely figured this one out by now: Having a child means tabling some of our other goals and ambitions, if only in order to preserve our energy and maintain our sanity.

But here's a rule of thumb: The trade-offs we make must be in keeping with our most deeply held values. If we're choosing to remain home and put our career on hold, that's great, but only as long as we're satisfied and fulfilled. If we're balancing career and children but sacrificing personal time or community involvements, that's fine, too, as long as we're comfortable with our choices.

And these choices change over time. What's important is to be at peace with what we have and what that says about who we are in the present, right now.

Affirmation: I know who I am and I know what matters most to me.

Peacekeeping

Parents are not interested in justice, they're interested in quiet.
Bill Cosby

Being a mother is a lot like being a referee—you're constantly called upon to arbitrate, and whatever call you make, somebody might read you the riot act.

Veteran moms offer this advice: Stay on the sidelines as much as possible. Whether it's figuring out whose turn it is on the swing set or mediating sibling-rivalry battles, the best call is to encourage kids to work it out themselves.

If you must get involved, assume a nonpartisan listening role. Because the more kids negotiate with one another, the better they get at learning to solve problems on their own.

Affirmation: I'll try to stand on the sidelines.

A Day in the Life

You've heard it's not damaging to let children cry themselves to sleep, but your eighteen-month-old daughter sobs uncontrollably unless you lie down next to her until she drifts off. You don't want to be her "security blanket." On the other hand you don't want her to feel abandoned. Do you just let her cry and cry and cry?

This is one of those situations that's at least as painful for mothers as for children. If we let our children cry, we feel guilty and upset; how can we justify ignoring our child when he or she needs us? But we also don't want to be controlled by our children; if we rush to their rescue, we worry they'll come to expect it and never learn how to comfort themselves.

Here's where persistence—and a good egg timer—and common sense come together. Decide how long it's okay for your child to cry—and how long *you* can stand it without bursting into tears yourself—and stick to your guns. You might start with thirty minutes. Give it a week. Whenever you're tempted to give in, repeat to yourself:

Affirmation: I'm helping my child learn how to go to sleep.

Family Vacations

There's no such thing as fun for the whole family.
Jerry Seinfeld

Family vacations seem to take on a mythic quality, especially before—when we're planning—and after when we're back home reminiscing over the photographs.

In between they often fall short of our fantasies. Why? Because vacations with kids simply aren't vacations, at least not in the way that we remember them from our own childhood. In the parent version we get very little rest, we spend most—if not all—our time doing what the kids want, *not* what we'd enjoy, and all too often we return home more exhausted than when we left.

Unless we're going to a family Club Med with round-the-clock child care or supervised kiddie activities, it's best to keep expectations in line. This is not an opportunity for rest and relaxation. Rather it's a way of making memories that your children—and someday even you—will look back on and treasure.

Affirmation: I'll rest when I get home.

Time-out

> *When my kids become wild and unruly, I use a nice, safe playpen. When they're finished, I climb out.*
> Erma Bombeck

As mothers we are constantly "shushing" our kids. It seems as if the longer we're parents, the lower our tolerance for noise and commotion.

All children are somewhat noisy, wild, and unruly. They're spirited, and thank goodness they are; we'd worry if they sat passively in a corner. Notice, for example, how thrilled and relieved we are when our child recovers from being ill and resumes making his usual ruckus.

Which doesn't necessarily make it easy or pleasant to listen to the uproar. At times we *do* need to remove ourselves temporarily. We take a short break or insist on mandatory quiet time—for them *and* for us—until we're ready to cope with their seemingly boundless energy.

Affirmation: I'm grateful for my child's energy.

Praise

I praise loudly; I blame softly.
Catherine II of Russia

Excellent advice to mothers. By praising loudly we build our children's self-esteem; by blaming softly we get our point across effectively and respectfully.

Too often we do exactly the opposite; we forget to praise our children—taking their good behavior and achievements for granted—while making too big a deal when they fall short of the mark. Shouting "Great job!" to the rooftops tells our children we appreciate and approve of their efforts. Whispering "This isn't the way to behave" tells our children what we expect without robbing them of their dignity.

Affirmation: A soft touch is often more effective.

At-Home Moms

> *If the women's movement did any harm at all, it gave the*
> *woman who stayed at home an inferiority complex.*
> *Barbara Walters*

Let's hear it for mothers at home with children.

Because Barbara Walters is right. For all the crucial advances the women's movement achieved, motherhood got the short end of the stick, often portrayed by feminists as a lowly, second-rate trap.

Happily many feminists now acknowledge mothering as an area of expertise and achievement for women. And hopefully, as more women are choosing—and are economically able—to remain home with children, motherhood as a "career" will be increasingly valued throughout society. Whatever our personal choice—whether we're at home with children or out in the world—we share the responsibility to grant motherhood the reverence it deserves.

Affirmation: Motherhood is a highly respectable occupation.

Growth

Babies don't need vacations but I still see them at the beach.
Steven Wright

Does it ever occur to you that babies have it better than anyone else? All they have to do is eat and sleep and be rocked and cuddled; we look at them, look at our to-do list, and wish we could trade places, even for an hour or two.

But appearances are deceiving. Our children are doing a great deal; they're incredibly busy growing, developing their personality, learning language, figuring out the mechanics of crawling, walking, drinking from a cup.

It may look like nothing compared with running a household or making a living. But their lives are every bit as exhausting—and challenging—just in a different way.

Affirmation: Even children work hard.

Wisdom

> *Wisdom is knowing when you can't be wise.*
> Paul Engle

It takes wisdom and humility to admit when we need help. When we don't have the answers. When we're not sure of the right thing to do.

Then it's important to seek support and assistance. From our pediatrician, child-development counselor, other professionals, or other parents who can share their experience and guide us in our journey.

We needn't ever be ashamed or embarrassed to ask for help. The wisdom to acknowledge our limits—and the willingness to stretch them—is all we need ask of ourselves as we continue to grow in our parenting.

Affirmation: I'm strong enough to ask for help.

Intimacy

For me, motherhood has been the one true, great and wholly successful romance.

        Irma Kurtz

Is there a mother anywhere on the planet who isn't deeply, passionately, madly in love with her child?

In some ways this may be the greatest romance of our lives. Our devotion transcends all other human connection; no one has more power than our children to make our hearts heavy with sorrow, expansive with joy.

At times it can seem as if our feelings toward our children are stronger, more intimate than our feelings toward our mate. Perhaps so, which is all the more reason to value—and attend to our marriage or relationship. The two relationships are utterly different and each is vastly important. We must always make sure to nurture the romance with the one person we'll grow old with when our children—as they will—grow up and find romance of their own.

Affirmation: I'll kindle the fires of my adult love relationship.

A Day in the Life

Your best friend just came over to tell you she's pregnant. She asks you what it's really like to be a mom. Speaking as the voice of experience, what do you say?

Do you tell her that so far it's been the greatest adventure of your life? Do you talk about how hard it is and how much work it involves? How can you possibly convey the intense mixture of love, fear, pride, vulnerability, apprehension, and excitement you've experienced—and continue to experience—now that you're a mother?

Even if no one has specifically asked you this question, this is a good opportunity to stop and take stock. Reflect back on the past year. What were the highlights? The low points? What strengths have you gained? What wisdom? What knowledge?

Ask yourself the question What *is* it like to be a mother?

Affirmation: So far being a mother is

_____.

Time

The walks and talks we have with our two-year-olds in red boots have a great deal to do with the values they will cherish as adults.

                    Edith F. Hunter

My friend Elana discovered that taking walks with her son, Noah, was the best way to get his undivided attention. "Life is so busy," she said, "but when we go for a walk, we finally have time to talk about all sorts of things . . . school, his friends, what he likes and dislikes . . . what's really going on inside."

I've discovered that baths are another great venue for talking with kids. Some of the best conversations I've had with my children have taken place while soaping their backs, sitting on the bathroom floor, or even soaking together in a nice, hot bubble bath.

As a rule kids open up when they don't have to compete for our attention.

Affirmation: Each day I'll make the time for uninterrupted talks with my child.

Meaning

> *Being a mother is what I think has made me the person I am.*
> Jacqueline Kennedy Onassis

These words from a woman who counts among her life experience having been First Lady, wife of a billionaire, world citizen, and successful book editor, just to name a few highlights.

Yet what does Jackie O. consider to be the most significant, life-shaping experience? Motherhood.

Actually I'm not surprised. No matter what else we achieve, being a mother shapes our character beyond anything else we undertake. The lessons we learn—patience, understanding, compassion, spiritual detachment—have a profound effect on who we become and how we carry ourselves in every other sphere of our lives.

Affirmation: We are forever changed through the experience of motherhood.

Nurturing

I felt about my children as if they were plants.
Jehan Sadat

And from another internationally renowned woman—
and wife of the late Egyptian president, Anwar Sadat—
come these sweet words on motherhood.

Like plants, our children need light and water, love and
gentle tending in order to flower. We illuminate their
lives through education and example. We nourish them
with healthful food and a nurturing environment. We
gently tend to their spirits by giving them love, consistent
guidance, perennial devotion.

Then we watch with pride as they blossom.

Affirmation: My child is a beautiful garden.

Togetherness

> *Grow up together, constantly.*
> Leo Buscaglia

A perfect blessing for parents and children. The process of parenting involves constant growth, not only for children but for parents as well. But in order to "grow up" together, we need to be open to learning, we need to have fun, and we need always to appreciate the strength of our love.

So here's what I'd add to Buscaglia's "blessing":

Learn together, constantly.
Laugh together, constantly.
Love together, constantly.

This is what it means to be a family. Together we learn and laugh and love and grow.

Affirmation: It's a blessing to grow with our children.

Hopes and Dreams

Every mother has a secret dream for her child.
Louise DeGrave

Our hopes and dreams evolve as we make the transition from pregnancy to childbirth to motherhood.

Now that you know your child, now that he or she is a tangible person you can see and touch and feel, what are your secret hopes and dreams? Do you dream of your children becoming actresses or astronauts? Do you dream of them coming of age in a secure and peaceful world? Do you dream of them someday having their own child and experiencing the joys of parenthood?

Every mother has her own dreams. What are yours?

Affirmation: My dream is for my child to

_____.

Guidance

> *My responsibility is to provide them a map, a lunch for the*
> *way and salve for bear scratches.*
> Ellen Walker

Ultimately this is what it comes down to: We provide
our children the signposts to help them travel their life's
journey safely and happily. We put their pacifier in their
baby bag, their eraser in their pencil box, a quarter to call
home when they're old enough to venture out on their
own.

And we're ready with salve for the bear scratches and
soothing words for the inevitable hurts. No matter where
they go or how old they get.

Affirmation: We will always be our child's mother.

Prayer

Pray to God. She will help you.
        Alva Vanderbilt Belmont

When all is said and done, there is always the power of prayer to help us through the ongoing struggles and challenges of motherhood.

Whether or not we're "religious," prayer, in whatever way it's expressed, comforts and strengthens us. As the Jewish saying goes, "All prayer is longing." Longing for guidance. Longing for courage. Longing for the wisdom required to give our children what they need.

Yet prayer is also a way of giving thanks. As we look at our child, there is so very, very much to be grateful for.

Affirmation: I offer prayers of gratitude for the joys of motherhood.

Love

> *A mother is someone who loves you.*
> *Evan Stern*

I leave you with these simple words from my son.

"But *why* does she love you?" I pressed Evan, trying to get him to elaborate. His answer: "Because you're her only eight-year-old son."

What more is there to say? When it comes right down to it, we don't love our children because they're pretty or smart or well behaved. We just love them because they're our children. And because we have the great privilege of being their mother. We love them fiercely. We love them completely. We love them forever.

Affirmation: I love you.

About the Author

Ellen Sue Stern is the author of *Expecting Change: The Emotional Journey Through Pregnancy; The Indispensable Woman; Shortchanged: What You Gain When You Choose to Love Him or Leave Him; Running on Empty: Meditations for Indispensable Women; I Do: Meditations for Newlyweds; I'm Having a Baby: Meditations for Expectant Mothers;* and *Questions Kids Wish They Could Ask Their Parents,* coauthored with Zoe Stern. Her work has appeared in *Self, New Woman, Parenting, Woman's Day,* and *American Baby* magazine, for which she writes a regular column. She has appeared on numerous television shows, including *The Oprah Winfrey Show, Maury Povich,* and *Sally Jessy Raphael.* Ellen Sue Stern lives in Minneapolis with her children, Zoe and Evan.

INDEX

Abandonment: Month 10, Day 26

Acceptance: Month 8, Day 17

Acknowledgement: Month 6, Day 25; Month 7, Day 1

Adjustments: Month 8, Day 23

Admiration: Month 1, Day 10

Adoption: Month 6, Day 27

Adoration: Month 5, Day 4

Advice: Month 1, Day 9

Affection: Month 5, Day 19; Month 7, Day 16; Month 12, Day 9

Ambition: Month 5, Day 16

Anger: Month 2, Day 5; Month 6, Day 2

Anxiety: Month 2, Day 2

Appreciation: Month 4, Day 28; Month 6, Day 19

Approval: Month 7, Day 26; Month 8, Day 12

Arguing: Month 9, Day 24

Arsenic Hour: Month 7, Day 17

At-Home Moms: Month 12, Day 18

Attention: Month 9, Day 8

Authority: Month 10, Day 4; Month 10, Day 27

Awareness: Month 8, Day 7

Baby-proofing: Month 8, Day 20

Baby Talk: Month 8, Day 30

Babysitters: Month 3, Day 12

Balance: Month 7, Day 27

Bathrooms: Month 11, Day 27

Bedtime: Month 8, Day 21

Beginnings: Month 2, Day 1

Being in Charge: Month 8, Day 28

Birds and Bees: Month 10, Day 22

Birth Day: Month 1, Day 1

Bonding: Month 1, Day 13

Boundaries: Month 2, Day 4

Busyness: Month 6, Day 14

Casualness: Month 5, Day 18

Cereal: Month 6, Day 30

Challenges: Month 3, Day 7; Month 6, Day 26

Changes: Month 4, Day 10

Child Care: Month 2, Day 25

Child Raising: Month 9, Day 17

Choices: Month 10, Day 14

Commitment: Month 3, Day 26; Month 4, Day 22

Compassion: Month 5, Day 23; Month 11, Day 20

Compensation: Month 4, Day 30

Conditioning: Month 2, Day 22

Confidences: Month 11, Day 29

Conscience: Month 11, Day 24

Consequences: Month 10, Day 5

Contributions: Month 10, Day 15

Control: Month 10, Day 8

Crawling: Month 6, Day 28

Creativity: Month 6, Day 17

Criticism: Month 8, Day 5; Month 11, Day 16

Cutting the Cord: Month 1, Day 3

Day in the Life: Month 1, Day 11; Month 1, Day 22; Month 2, Day 13; Month 2, Day 26; Month 3, Day 11; Month 3, Day 23; Month 4, Day 11; Month 4, Day 21; Month 5, Day 12; Month 5, Day 22; Month 6, Day 12; Month 6, Day 22; Month 7, Day 13; Month 7, Day 23; Month 8, Day 13; Month 8, Day 25; Month 9, Day 13; Month 9, Day 23; Month 10, Day 12; Month 10, Day 23; Month 11, Day 12; Month 11, Day 22; Month 12, Day 14; Month 12, Day 22

Delegating: Month 5, Day 25; Month 9, Day 28

Dependency: Month 6, Day 10; Month 10, Day 29

Depression: Month 6, Day 7

Devotion: Month 3, Day 5

"Difficult" Kids: Month 5, Day 28

Diplomacy: Month 4, Day 17

Discipline: Month 4, Day 3

Discovery: Month 4, Day 12; Month 8, Day 18

Distraction: Month 8, Day 10

Eating Out: Month 11, Day 18

Education: Month 5, Day 6; Month 10, Day 24

Emotional Security: Month 10, Day 16

Emotions: Month 1, Day 8

Empowerment: Month 4, Day 29

Encouragement: Month 8, Day 15

Equal Opportunity: Month 9, Day 9

Equal Parenting: Month 1, Day 30; Month 7, Day 20

Evolution: Month 9, Day 3

Exasperation: Month 7, Day 25

Exhaustion: Month Five, Day 1; Month 9, Day 2

Expectations: Month 2, Day 19; Month 9, Day 21

Expenses: Month 5, Day 9; Month 10, Day 3

Expression: Month 9, Day 29

Faith: Month 6, Day 5

Family Jokes: Month 6, Day 8

Family Vacations: Month 12, Day 15

Fantasies: Month 8, Day 22

Fatherhood: Month 8, Day 8

Fathers: Month 3, Day 2; Month 7, Day 3

Fear: Month 1, Day 5; Month 6, Day 15

Firstborns: Month 1, Day 12; Month 8, Day 11

Flexibility: Month 3, Day 1; Month 6, Day 3

Food: Month 4, Day 14

Friendship: Month 8, Day 24

Frustration: Month 4, Day 26

Gifts: Month 7, Day 11; Month 10, Day 11

Giving: Month 1, Day 18

Giving In: Month 4, Day 8

Going Out: Month 5, Day 10

Graciousness: Month 6, Day 16

Grandparents: Month 3, Day 22; Month 4, Day 18

Gratitude: Month 9, Day 4; Month 11, Day 1

Grocery-shopping: Month 10, Day 7

Grounding: Month 7, Day 6; Month 9, Day 10

Growing Up: Month 6, Day 1

Growth: Month 12, Day 19

Guidance: Month 12, Day 28

Guilt: Month 6, Day 21; Month 10, Day 28

Hands: Month 9, Day 12

Hard Days: Month 8, Day 3

Helplessness: Month 9, Day 15

Home: Month 5, Day 20

Honesty: Month 3, Day 18; Month 7, Day 30; Month 9, Day 22; Month 11, Day 13

Hopes and Dreams: Month 12, Day 27

Housecleaning: Month 2, Day 18; Month 9, Day 7

Humility: Month 2, Day 3; Month 5, Day 14

Humor: Month 3, Day 24

Idealization: Month 6, Day 6

Improvisation: Month 5, Day 2

Independence: Month 2, Day 16

Individuation: Month 6, Day 11

Infancy: Month 7, Day 15

Influence: Month 4, Day 4; Month 9, Day 27

Ingenuity: Month 3, Day 3

Inner Child: Month 4, Day 25

Inner Strength: Month 11, Day 19

Innocence: Month 10, Day 10

Intelligence: Month 10, Day 9

Intensity: Month 3, Day 13

Interruptions: Month 2, Day 20

Intimacy: Month 1, Day 6; Month 12, Day 21

Inventiveness: Month 4, Day 1

Joy: Month 5, Day 30

Juggling: Month 1, Day 20

Language: Month 4, Day 13

Legacies: Month 3, Day 9

Lessons: Month 9, Day 26

Letting Go of Control: Month 1, Day 24

Lightening Up: Month 4, Day 16

Limitations: Month 9, Day 15

Limits: Month 10, Day 27

Listening: Month 11, Day 3

Little Things: Month 12, Day 11

Love: Month 2, Day 10; Month 7, Day 7; Month 12, Day 30

Lovemaking: Month 9, Day 30

Loving: Month 9, Day 1

Lullabies: Month 2, Day 30

Making Memories: Month 7, Day 22

Manners: Month 5, Day 24; Month 7, Day 18; Month 11, Day 2

Martyrdom: Month 5, Day 27

Meals: Month 2, Day 8

Meaning: Month 12, Day 24

Memories: Month 1, Day 7; Month 6, Day 23

Mentoring: Month 9, Day 6

Messes: Month 5, Day 15; Month 7, Day 10

Middle-of-the-Night Feedings: Month 1, Day 19

Milestones: Month 7, Day 24

Mistakes: Month 4, Day 27

Monsters: Month 7, Day 29

Mood Swings: Month 3, Day 15

Mornings: Month 12, Day 7

Mother's Day: Month 5, Day 5

Nagging: Month 1, Day 23; Month 9, Day 25

Noise: Month 8, Day 9

Nursing: Month 1, Day 16; Month 6, Day 13

Nurturing: Month 9, Day 5; Month 12, Day 25

Nutrition: Month 3, Day 28

Obedience: Month 10, Day 21

Ordinariness: Month 8, Day 6

Overprotectiveness: Month 7, Day 4; Month 11, Day 25

Overscheduling: Month 8, Day 4

Paradoxes: Month 7, Day 14

Parenting Styles: Month 4, Day 6

Patience: Month 3, Day 17; Month 5, Day 13; Month 9, Day 16; Month 9, Day 25

Peacekeeping: Month 12, Day 13

Pediatricians: Month 8, Day 29

Perfectionism: Month 3, Day 10

Permanence: Month 2, Day 6

Personal Growth: Month 2, Day 17; Month 7, Day 19

Playfulness: Month 4, Day 2

PMS: Month 12, Day 5

Postpartum: Month 4, Day 24

Power: Month 6, Day 4

Praise: Month 7, Day 9; Month 12, Day 17

Prayer: Month 12, Day 29

Precociousness: Month 11, Day 21

Preoccupation: Month 1, Day 15

Preparation: Month 11, Day 17

Presents: Month 8, Day 19

Pressure: Month 5, Day 3; Month 11, Day 28; Month 12, Day 10

Priorities: Month 11, Day 8; Month 12, Day 12

Privacy: Month 3, Day 21; Month 10, Day 13; Month 12, Day 3

Problems: Month 5, Day 21

Protectiveness: Month 2, Day 29

Pushing: Month 5, Day 29

Quality Time: Month 2, Day 9; Month 10, Day 19

Real Life: Month 11, Day 11

Realism: Month 10, Day 1

Reassurance: Month 5, Day 7; Month 12, Day 6

Rebelliousness: Month 11, Day 6

Rejoicing: Month 11, Day 26

Respect: Month 1, Day 17; Month 6, Day 29; Month 7, Day 28

Responsibility: Month 4, Day 15; Month 8, Day 27; Month 11, Day 9

Returning to "Work": Month 2, Day 23

Risks: Month 4, Day 19

Role Models: Month 9, Day 14; Month 12, Day 1

Roots: Month 6, Day 20

Rules: Month 3, Day 29

Sacrifice: Month 3, Day 19

Sanctuary: Month 6, Day 9

Savings: Month 10, Day 18

Scolding: Month 2, Day 11

Self-acceptance: Month 1, Day 14; Month 9, Day 11

Self-actualization: Month 2, Day 21; Month 11, Day 5

Self-appreciation: Month 2, Day 15; Month 4, Day 25

Self-care: Month 3, Day 20

Self-discovery: Month 3, Day 16

Self-forgiveness: Month 7, Day 12

Self-preservation: Month 8, Day 1

Self-trust: Month 9, Day 18

Sensitivity: Month 1, Day 21

Sensuality: Month 3, Day 14

Setting an Example: Month 3, Day 25

Setting Limits: Month 2, Day 14

Sexism: Month 9, Day 9

Sharing: Month 1, Day 27; Month 4, Day 5

Shlepping: Month 3, Day 6

Sibling Rivalry: Month 3, Day 4; Month 7, Day 2

Sickness: Month 11, Day 7

Silliness: Month 5, Day 17

Simple Pleasures: Month 2, Day 27

Single Moms: Month 3, Day 27

Skill Building: Month 5, Day 11

Skills: Month 8, Day 2

Sleep: Month 1, Day 25

Slowing Down: Month 10, Day 20

Smiles: Month 4, Day 9; Month 8, Day 16

Social Activism: Month 9, Day 19

Solitude: Month 11, Day 23

Spontaneity: Month 8, Day 26

Staying Calm: Month 2, Day 7

Stickiness: Month 1, Day 26

Stimulation: Month 4, Day 7

Struggling: Month 7, Day 8

Supermom: Month 2, Day 28; Month 11, Day 4

Support: Month 6, Day 18; Month 4, Day 24

Tantrums: Month 10, Day 25

Taste: Month 5, Day 8

Tears: Month 9, Day 20

Teething: Month 3, Day 30

Tenderness: Month 3, Day 8

Terror: Month 2, Day 12

The First Cry: Month 1, Day 2

Threats: Month 5, Day 26

Time: Month 12, Day 23

Time-out: Month 12, Day 16

Time Passing: Month 11, Day 30

Timing: Month 4, Day 20

Togetherness: Month 12, Day 26

Tolerance: Month 8, Day 14; Month 11, Day 10

Toys: Month 12, Day 8

Trial and Error: Month 4, Day 23

TV: Month 11, Day 15

Ungratefulness: Month 10, Day 6

Values: Month 11, Day 14

Visitors: Month 1, Day 28

Vocabulary: Month 2, Day 24

Vulnerability: Month 6, Day 24

Weaning: Month 7, Day 21

Weight Loss: Month 1, Day 4

Wholeness: Month 12, Day 2

Wisdom: Month 7, Day 5; Month 12, Day 20

"Working Mothers": Month 1, Day 29; Month 10, Day 17

Worries: Month 12, Day 4